The

Sound *RIDER!*

guide to

Motorcycling in the Columbia River Gorge

by Tom Mehren

Mixed *MEDIA*

2226 Eastlake Avenue East, Suite 69
Seattle, WA 98102
www.mm411.com

*This third edition is dedicated to my tech of 10 years, Andy Moore,
the person who's made it possible for me to ride thousands of flawless
miles on my bikes in The Gorge area since 2000.*

Mixed *MEDIA* PRODUCTION TEAM

Publisher
Tom Mehren

Editing
Connie Adams, Patrick Duff

Layout & Design
Tom Mehren, Patrick Duff

Cartography
Tim Pizzino, Ryan Barnett

Pre Riders
*Tom Mehren, Bruce Scott, Harvey Gilkerson, Jim Palms, Vernon
Wade, Bob Tomlinson*

3rd Edition Printing
Gorham Printing, Centralia WA

Special thanks to Connie, Harvey Gilkerson, Jim Palms, Bruce Scott,
Vernon Wade, Bob Tomlinson, Mike Hew, David Hough, Danielle
Scoggins, Tamara Timmons, Kurt Gorham, Fox & Dana and everyone
at the Skamania Chamber and Skamania Facilities & Recreation

All photos by Tom Mehren except where noted.
All content Copyright ©2004, 2006, 2008 Mixed *MEDIA*

All rights reserved. This book may not be duplicated or transmitted in any form by way
of photocopying, recording, mechanical or electronic copying, or any other means
without written consent of the publisher. The author and publisher assume no liability
for any errors or omissions that may exist and the damages that may result from the use
of this information. Both the author and the publisher of the Sound *RIDER!* guide to
Motorcycling in the Columbia River Gorge disclaim any and all responsibility for the
incursion of personal or other than personal liabilities and risk from the application or
direct or indirect use of any of the contents of this book.

Table of Contents

Introduction...*4*

History of The Gorge...*6*

Motorcycling in The Gorge...*10*

The Pavement Rides...*14*

Dualsporting in The Gorge...*52*

The Dualsport Rides...*57*

Commonsense Riding Practices...*85*

Tips & Tricks...*101*

See & Do...*106*

Where to Eat...*110*

Where to Stay...*120*

Creating Poker Runs in The Gorge...*126*

Ride Index...*128*

Introduction

Travel guides have a way of getting crusty after a few years. Places change names, new things sprout up here and there and technology brings advances that change the way we navigate a ride.

So here we are at the third edition of our Gorge guide and to me it's the best yet. We've added a number of new rides, reworked every map and every set of directions, changed a few routes here and there to offer better vantage points along the rides and to accommodate those never-ending gravel road closures that dualsport riders must endure.

After riding the area for eight years you'd think we'd probably been everywhere there is to go, but it never ceases to amaze me how each year I stumble across a few new roads every time I go. Looking over my atlas, there are still several roads on my list to try out, don't expect this to be the last edition.

After holding a number of motorcycle rallies in The Gorge since 2003 (www.soundrider.com/rally), we've had time to look over the most common crash occurrences and how to avoid them. We've added an entire chapter that will hopefully aid in crash reduction whether you're at one of the rallies or just enjoying a weekend with friends in the region. Most of the situations apply to wherever you ride, not just The Gorge.

Don't blame it on us, but since we've been promoting The Gorge as a great place to ride over the years via this book, our rallies and in our Sound *RIDER!* online magazine, riding popularity in the area has increased. We're seeing more and more riders in the area each year. Places like Stevenson, Hood River and Goldendale all rely heavily on tourist business to keep their economy healthy so your visit is welcome by the local businesses. The lesson here is you may want to plan ahead to be certain you get the accommodations you want to stay and a table at your favorite restaurant. In general The Gorge region is hosting more and more events in the summer months that fill up hotel rooms and restaurants, making it more of a gamble if you think you'll just roll into town without having made reservations ahead of time.

To assist you with your trip planning, this new edition also includes listings of our favorite accommodations and tried-and-true restaurant locations that have stood the test of time and our palates.

We've also taken a section of the book to discuss poker runs. If you don't know what one is, read the chapter. Designing simple poker runs is a great way to link together rides in this book and have a little fun while you're out enjoying the scenic beauty and never-ending twisties.

A word about the odometer notes in the directions. Your odometer readings will no doubt vary. Many motorcycles can have up to a seven percent variance in accuracy. Use the odometer notes as a basis for knowing where you are and to determine distance between points, but don't expect them to match yours exactly because they probably won't. They come to us fresh from the propeller heads at NAVTEQ and have proven very accurate when ridden with a GPS.

Dig in, enjoy all this book and The Gorge have to offer, again and again. I have yet to meet anyone who did it all in one trip. Ride well.

History of The Gorge

As long as you're going to ride in The Gorge area, it's good to know a little bit about the place. The Columbia River Gorge is an area rich in history going back to the last ice age. Ever since then it's been a changing area geologically, politically and agriculturally. How did it come to be, and more importantly, how did it become a world-class motorcycling area?

Back at the end of the last ice age, Montana played host to glaciers as the Cordilleran Ice Sheet receded and eventually began to melt and turn into lakes surrounded by glacial dams. In other words, dams made of ice. Welcome to the birth of global warming. Eventually the dams broke as the earth heated up. The Missoula floods were created sending a gazillion gallons of water westward several times carving some serious canyons, rivers and terrain along the way. The Columbia River Gorge was one such recipient of this liquid deluge.

Fast forward to the time before Lewis & Clark when Native Americans populated the region, living off the land. What a pleasant and peaceful place it must have been. Spear a fish for breakfast, bow and arrow a rabbit for dinner, tan a few hides and you've had a full work day.

Then in the 1800s, the U.S. military sent Lewis & Clark westward to see what the area

Sam Hill: Photo courtesy of the Maryhill Museum

6

was all about. The pair reported back what a great place it was. Rich in wildlife, minerals and other natural resources, it wasn't long before the Oregon trail was ablaze with new settlers. At this point, the Native Americans were sequestered, locks and dams were built, train tracks were laid and it was onward to the industrial revolution.

By the turn of the century, the automobile was on the horizon and roads needed to be built and paved. Enter Sam Hill. A wealthy attorney, Hill made his home in both Seattle and near Goldendale in an area he named after his daughter Mary, Maryhill. Hill was enamored by the invention of the automobile and saw the need for paved roads well before many others. He tested road building on his property in Maryhill, building the first paved road in

The Bridge of the Gods spans the Columbia River at the Cascade Locks. The area was changed greatly from a landslide that occurred hundreds of years ago. When the Bonneville Dam was built, the bridge had to be raised some 30-odd feet above it's original location.

the state, the Maryhill Loops road, which is still there but closed to vehicles today. Hill showed his road to the then Governor of Washington State seeking to build what is now SR 14. Hill was denied the request. Meanwhile, Oregon thought it would be a grand idea to build a paved road from Portland out east and together Sam Hill and engineer Sam Lancaster built the Columbia River Gorge Highway. Hill took Lancaster and his staff to Europe to show them what was being done there. Thus the elegant bridges and, more importantly, the Vista House took shape. Hill probably had no idea what fun you would have on your motorcycle here, but most say he'd be pleased with the results of modern-day machines pushing the limits of the pavement.

The advent of I-84 terminated many sections of the Columbia River Highway, as did the creation of several dams. What we have left today are some of the finer sections of road such as the stretch from Multnomah Falls to Troutdale, and the scenic Rowena Plateau segment from Mosier to the Dalles. Fine motorcycling roads if ever

US 30 at Rowena Plateau circa 1917. The road design stays the same today. Sweet!

there were.

As you ride through The Gorge, you'll notice a distinct difference in the climate from west to east. A moist, cool coastal climate on the west side gives way to the easterly dry region just around The Dalles.

The hillsides change from lush green trees full of deer, to scrub brush and rocks hosting snakes and prairie varmints with one thing tying the whole deal together – the Columbia River.

The Gorge has a diverse agricultural palette. Fruit, grains, wine grapes and more are grown here. The Mosier area is one of the largest Maraschino cherry regions in the world. Hood River is one of the largest Bartlett pear regions in the world. Grapes were recently introduced from Maryhill to Bingen, and the Washington wine boom is in full swing here as well.

Playing on your motorcycle is just one of the many recreational activities in the area. You'll see plenty of windsurfers as you ride, particularly near Hood River, the wind surfing capital of the world. There are also hikers, campers, rock climbers and plenty of bicyclists enjoying all The Gorge has to offer. Here you're at the lowest elevation of the Cascade range with the Pacific Trail passing through at Cascade Locks.

As you ride your motorcycle through the region, you can't help but notice the geologic occurrences from lava flows to glacial carving, from the land slides to the wind and water-shaped canyon walls. To put it simply, Wind Mountain just east of Stevenson, as large as it is, is nothing more than a tiny volcanic plug sitting on top of a large volcano, now buried, that existed before that first Missoula flood arrived.

The Gorge is a big beautiful playground for you to enjoy on your motorcycle. Have a great time.

Motorcycling in The Gorge

The Gorge and its surrounding areas make for a world-class riding area. But it's not as if foreigners are flocking here to ride. Little has been written about riding in the area, and today it still remains a region well under radar in comparison to other places like Switzerland and New Zealand.

My first adventure into The Gorge by motorcycle came in the year 2000 when I arrived by way of SR 14 from the west side in the late afternoon. The sun was illuminating everything with an orange glow and it reminded me of the first time I went to Yosemite in California. When I reached North Bonneville, I watched a deer jump a barbed wire fence. Many people have tried to change the way things are in The Gorge, but the deer made a good point - nature will always find a way around what man has done.

Having spent so much time riding the area since

then, there's just one thing that most travelers will figure out after several days here. There's a lot to see and do and you can't cram it into a few days. Alas, you must return again later and conquer the other rides and sights you missed before.

Things to keep in mind

THE LEGAL STUFF

Washington and Oregon both require you to have a current endorsement on your driver's license to operate a motorcycle. They also require you that wear a helmet when you ride. In addition, Oregon requires that you carry proof of insurance specific to your motorcycle.

WEATHER

Being that this area lies smack dab in the middle of the Cascade mountain range and comes with several climate types, The Gorge is always whipping up it's own brew of weather that changes daily. Even in the summer, a beautiful warm day can turn into a wind guster complete with rain and hail in a short amount of time. Always pack several layers of clothing and always bring rain gear.

GRATED BRIDGES

There are two notorious grated bridges in The Gorge – Bridge of the Gods and the Hood River bridge. Keep at or below the posted speed limit as you cross and you'll greatly reduce your chances of an incident. If the wind is up, ride with extra caution and don't cross if you're not comfortable doing so. My own experience has shown that Avon Tyres Sport Touring treads are the least squirrelly on grated bridges in comparison to other brands such as Michelin and Dunlop.

The grated bridges also carry a toll in both

11

directions. While small, it's a pain in the butt reaching into your pocket for a few coins each time you cross. Plan to place a few in easier-to-reach places like your tank bag.

The bridges at The Dalles (US 197) and Goldendale (US 97) are paved and there are no tolls.

CAMPING

Motorcycle camping isn't nearly as popular in the Northwest as it is with our Canadian neighbors. However, if you're on a budget and don't mind sleeping under the stars, it's a fine alternative to a spendy hotel or a cheap motel.

But there's one thing that must be remembered about The Gorge before laying your body down at the end of the day – there are trains here that run 24 hours a day! Pretty much anywhere you camp in The Gorge you will hear trains. Bring ear plugs (I hope you're wearing them whenever you ride already) and use them at bedtime.

The other alternative is to camp up yonder at a myriad of campgrounds that can be accessed in both Washington and Oregon. Areas such as the the Wind River, Hood River and Trout Lake areas all sport several campgrounds each from the roar of the trains.

A listing of some favorite sites is included in the back of this book.

MOTELS

There are motels in key cities throughout The Gorge including Stevenson, Hood River, Cascade Locks and The Dalles. Getting into one on a weekday or non-summer weekend is never too tough. However, in the summer the region hosts a plethora of activities and rooms go fast, so it's best to plan ahead and make advance reservations. Check the back of the book for a variety of trusted places.

HOTELS AND RESORTS

There are several hotels and resorts in the area if you're looking to pamper yourself when you're not in the saddle. For a bit of historical charm, consider the Hood River Hotel in Hood River or The Edgefield in Troutdale. For a spa sensation check out the Bonneville Hot Springs Resort in North Bonneville, or the Carson Hot Springs Resort in Carson. If you like Yosemite's Awahnee Hotel, check out Skamania Lodge in Stevenson for a modern day version. Check the back of the book for some of our favorites.

DINING OUT

There's no shortage of good food in The Gorge. Each major population center comes complete with its share of inexpensive, mid-priced and expensive eateries. We've listed some of the better places that have been around three years or more further back in the book.

BIKING & HIKING

There are quite a few places to go hiking in The Gorge. A cable lock and some hiking shoes are the accessories you need to lock down your riding gear and climb a wonder such as Beacon Rock or Dog Mountain. Check the Sound *RIDER!* store online for the latest gear security items available for riders.

THE RIDES

Mosier Loop
**DISTANCE: 80 MILES
(40 MILES EACH DIRECTION)
RIDING TIME: ABOUT AN HOUR EACH WAY**

This loop ride takes you along miles of twisties just west of The Dalles. The area is a favorite for automotive commercial shoots and as a testing ground for auto and motorcycle editors from around the country. In August 2004, the area was used extensively for shooting the new Mercedes SLK sports model. In 2003, it was used by Yamaha to take product shots for the FZ-6. The list goes on and on. Scenic and twisty, it's a favorite for motorcyclists as well.

The route is such a blast in both directions that the length is listed as 80 miles, but it's actually 40 miles in each direction. Once you complete it counter-clockwise, head back out and do it again clockwise.

Begin by gassing up in nearby Hood River, then ride to Mosier just five miles east. Leave town by way of Oregon Sreet and 3rd Avenue. 3rd turns into State road and the twisties begin. You travel across the

14

top of Seven Mile Hill and get some breathtaking views of The Gorge below. Once you arrive at the bottom of the hill, you'll head south through the Browns Creek area and then it's back uphill onto the geologic flow of Cherry Hill Heights. One might assume this is where you go to live if you're one of the hob knobbing elitists from The Dalles. Note the Deer Crossing sign and sniff. During routing in August 2004, there was a distinct odor of dead carcasses along this stretch. It's a reminder of how careful you need to be while riding here. Once you descend into the Dalles, head west on 6th/SR 30 and ascend into some of the finest riding terrain you've ever tasted – The Rowena Plateau.

Yum Yum! Riders often pull out at the top, take a look at the road below, then turn the bike around and spend time going back and forth along the stretch from top to bottom until they've had enough. Once you've done that, continue west on US 30 to Mosier along more great pavement, take a break and then do the route in reverse. A real treat!

While you're on break between directions, be sure to visit the Route 30 auto museum and ice cream shop and lap up a little James Dean history.

The road as it wraps its way around a 270-degree sweeper at Rowena Plateau. Note the Euro-style guardrail designed by Sam Hill and Samuel Lancaster that dates back to the road's original construction in 1917. The Gorge lies below.

MOSIER LOOP DIRECTIONS

ODO	Instructions
0.0	Depart Mosier on Oregon St (South)
0.1	Turn LEFT (East) onto 3rd Ave
0.6	Road name changes to State Rd
0.6	Road name changes to Pioneer Rd [State Rd]
2.8	Road name changes to Old Mosier Rd [Pioneer Rd]
4.8	Bear LEFT (South) onto Old Mosier Rd [State Rd]
5.7	Road name changes to Seven Mile Hill Rd
11.7	Turn RIGHT (West) onto Chenoweth Creek Rd
13.6	Turn LEFT (South) onto Browns Creek Rd
17.1	Road name changes to Cherry Heights Rd
23.6	Turn LEFT (North-West) onto W 6th St (US 30)
25.5	Keep STRAIGHT onto US 30
34.0	Rowena Curves Overlook on LEFT
40.0	Arrive near Mosier

Another fine example of why this area is truly a world class motorcycling destination. Looking onto Highway 30 from atop the Rowena Plateau.

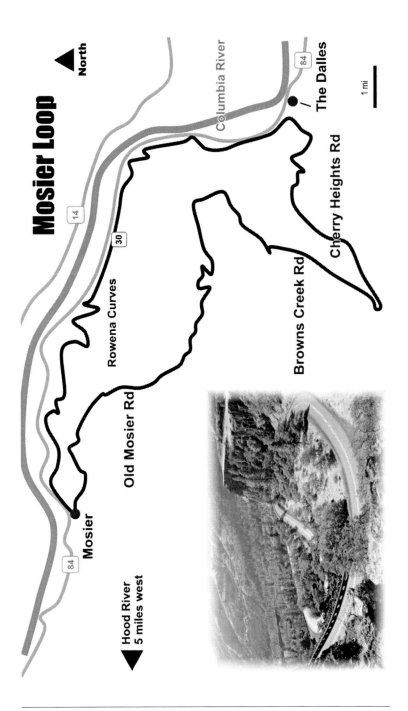

Mt. Hood Scenic Loop
DISTANCE: 151 MILES
RIDING TIME: ABOUT 4.25 HOURS

It would be easy to go for a ride around Mt. Hood via the main highways that surround it, but if you're looking for something a little less traveled, a bit more scenic and lots more fun, you'll get it with this ride. This loop takes you along every cow town road I could find from Hood River to Corbett. Along the way you'll see farmland, pear orchards and, of course, stunning views of Mt. Hood. I route this clockwise so you can begin in the late morning, enjoy lunch at Mt. Hood, then return westward getting plenty of good photo-op light on the mountain no matter where you are on the route. Bring a few layers of clothing. It could be 90 degrees in The Gorge when you leave, but only 60 degrees on top of Mt. Hood. Beginning this ride at around 10 a.m. will put you on Mt. Hood during lunch hour.

The route begins by leaving Stevenson heading east along SR 14. After 20 miles, take SR 35 onto the Hood River toll bridge. The bridge grating is some of the nastiest and if the wind is up it's a bit more challenging. Stick with the posted speed limit. You'll drive into Hood River, the Wind Surfing capitol of the world. If you haven't seen a wind surfer yet, there must not be any wind for miles. In summer of 2004 even, presidential contender John Kerry wind surfed here.

Leaving the city, you'll make your way southwest for a scenic view of the entire fruit farmland area and Mt. Hood from Panorama point. Then it's off to Parkdale for a romp along the Cooper Spur Road.

At the end you'll be spilled back onto SR 35 where you'll turn right and make your way to Timberline Lodge

18

on Mt. Hood. The six miles of twisties along Timberline Road are a two-wheel treat where you'll ascend another 2,000 feet to 6,000 feet above sea level at the lodge. If you get stuck behind a tour bus, pull out and give it time to get ahead so you can enjoy the stretch without any traffic in front of you. Lunch at Timberline Lodge is highly recommended. Gas up below at Government Camp as the next gas/restroom on the route isn't for another 50 miles.

The second part of the ride begins by heading west on Highway 26, but not for long. When you see the sign for the Lolo Pass turnout, take it and get ready for another long stretch of twisties with little traffic. You'll zigzag your way through Rhododendron, along Barlow Road, the Oregon Trail route out toward Bull Run along a series of nice two-lane roads. The roads between Bull Run and Corbett provide a look into the local farming communities.

Gas can be had in Corbett at the town store, but don't blink or you'll miss it. From Corbett, head east along the old Columbia River Highway. Take a break at the beautiful Vista House and get a bird's eye view of The Gorge below. Then descend into the trees along a series of waterfalls, most notable being Multnomah Falls. Your ride ends with a stretch back on I-84 and over the Bridge of the Gods.

The view of Mt. Hood with the Hood River Bridge in the foreground.

MT. HOOD SCENIC LOOP DIRECTIONS

ODO	Instructions
0.0	Depart Stevenson, WA on SR 14 [NE 2nd St] (East)
21.0	Turn RIGHT (South) onto Hood River Bridge
22.1	Turn RIGHT (West) onto US 30 [SR 35]
22.4	Turn LEFT (East) onto Old Columbia River Dr
22.9	Turn RIGHT (South-East) onto Riverview Dr
23.3	Turn RIGHT (West) onto Highline Rd
24.2	Bear LEFT (East) onto Eastside Rd
24.9	Panorama Point on RIGHT
27.5	Keep STRAIGHT onto Van Horn Dr
28.4	Turn LEFT (South) onto SR 35 [Mt Hood Hwy]
37.3	Bear RIGHT (South-West) onto Cooper Spur Rd
39.1	Bear LEFT (South) onto Cooper Spur Rd
49.5	Turn RIGHT (South) onto SR 35 [Mt Hood Hwy]
65.5	Turn RIGHT onto Ramp
65.9	Keep STRAIGHT onto US 26 [Mt Hood Hwy]
68.0	Turn RIGHT (North-East) onto Timberline Hwy
73.5	Arrive Timberline Lodge, return South on Timberline Hwy
78.8	Bear RIGHT (West) onto US 26 [Mt Hood Hwy]
90.6	Turn RIGHT (North) onto E Lolo Pass Rd [FS 18]
91.8	Turn LEFT (West) onto E Barlow Trail Rd
98.5	Turn RIGHT (North-West) onto E Marmot Rd
108.1	Turn LEFT to stay on E Marmot Rd
109.7	Turn RIGHT (North) onto SE Ten Eyck Rd
111.1	Turn RIGHT (East) onto SE Bull Run Rd
114.1	Turn LEFT to stay on SE Bull Run Rd
115.5	Road name changes to SE Gordon Creek Rd
122.1	Road name changes to (SE) Evans Rd
124.1	Turn RIGHT (East) onto SE Crown Point Hwy [Historic Columbia River Hwy]
126.2	Bear LEFT to stay on Historic Columbia River Hwy
139.3	Turn RIGHT (East) onto NE Frontage Rd [Historic Columbia River Hwy]
141.4	Take Ramp onto I-84 [US 30]
147.3	At exit 44, turn RIGHT onto Ramp
147.7	Bear RIGHT (North) onto US 30 [Wa-Na-Pa St]
147.7	Turn RIGHT onto Bridge of the Gods
148.4	Turn RIGHT (East) onto SR 14 [Evergreen Hwy]
151.0	Arrive Stevenson

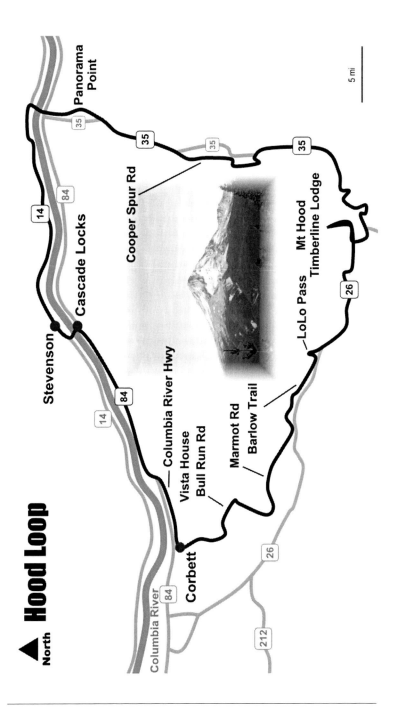

Twisties, Dinner & A Star Show
DISTANCE: 85 MILES
RIDING TIME: 2.5 HOURS

Imagine taking a long ride along some twisties, relaxing with a small town dinner and then having a look at the stars through one of the largest publicly-accessed telescopes west of the Rockies. It can be done.

Begin this trip about 4 hours before sunset so as to allow yourself enough time to ride and eat before the star show begins. Your destination, the Goldendale Observatory, opens to the public at dusk and is open in the summer Wednesday through Sunday.

For this trip we'll head east to the town of Goldendale with the sun at our backs through scenic forests, along the walls of the upper Klickitat Canyon and finally into the town of Goldendale for dinner and the star show.

Begin heading east on SR 14. At the junction of SR 141, turn left and head north until your get to BZ's Corner. Here you'll turn right and begin a roller coaster ride upward and along the Camas Prairie. The next town you reach will be Glenwood. Turn right and follow the main street east and southeast. It soon becomes the Goldendale-Glenwood Road.

In this section you will note you are on the west side of Klickitat Canyon, that is until the road descends and you ride across the bottom of a narrow section of canyon to the east wall. Here you begin a windy ascent upwards. The rock walls and stunning views have a way of stealing your attention so take it easy here and enjoy.

Soon you arrive on a farmland plateau just west of Goldendale. Turn left onto SR 142 and proceed east into

Goldendale. Upon arrival you'll find dining right in downtown, or on the east edge near Highway 97. We don't have any particular recommendations as names and places change over time. Simply take about 10 minutes to investigate and pick your spot.

After dinner, make your way a little west of downtown and follow the signs up to the Goldendale Observatory in the hills on the north side of town. Park Ranger Steve Stout puts on an informative show that makes it worth the trip out. If the weather is cooperating that evening, Stout will open the roof and everyone gets a chance to stargaze through the Cassegrain lens. Admission is free and a donation valued at the price of a trip to the movies or greater is highly recommended.

For the return ride home, we recommend heading south on Hwy 97 to SR 14 heading west back to home base. Riding back via Klickitat Canyon is not advised as it can be an outright deer farm in the dark and the roads don't lend themselves well to nighttime driving.

TWISTIES, DINNER & A STAR SHOW DIRECTIONS

ODO **Instructions**
- 0.0 Depart Stevenson on SR 14 [NE 2nd St] (East)
- 19.4 Turn LEFT (North) onto SR 141 Alt
- 21.6 Bear LEFT (North-West) onto SR 141
- 29.4 Turn RIGHT (North-East) onto BZ-Glenwood Hwy
- 29.6 At 70 BZ-Glenwood Hwy, White Salmon, WA stay on BZ-Glenwood Hwy (North-East)
- 49.0 Turn RIGHT (East) onto E Main St
- 49.5 Road name changes to Glenwood-Goldendale Rd [Goldendale Hwy]
- 73.2 Turn LEFT (East) onto SR 142
- 83.9 Turn LEFT (North) onto N Columbus Ave
- 84.5 Keep RIGHT onto Observatory Dr
- 85.3 Arrive Observatory

Twisties, Dinner & A Starshow

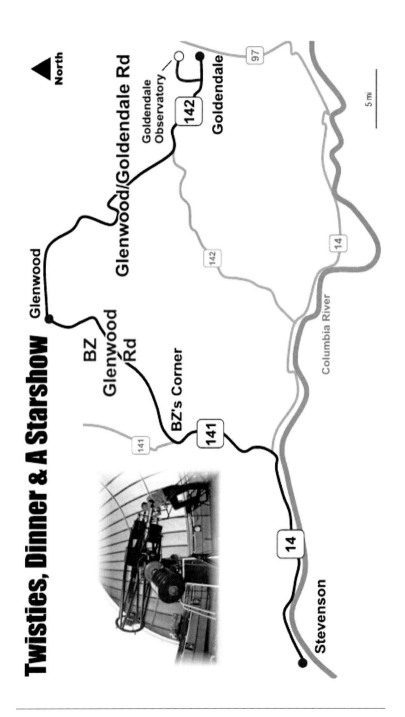

Three Rivers Loop
DISTANCE: 138 MILES
RIDING TIME: 4 HOURS

Lots of visitors to The Gorge have heard about what a grand motorcycling road the Wind River Road can be. But then what? Some continue to Mt. St. Helens, but if you're staying in The Gorge, it's a long day in the saddle. So I came up with the Three Rivers Loop. The ride takes you along three scenic rivers, gives you a great look at Mt. St. Helens and takes you through some small towns along a number of scenic roads. It's all here, the scenery, the cozy townships and, of course, the twisties...

Do the loop in any direction you like. The recommended route here is counterclockwise starting off in the morning. This way you'll have sun beaming onto Mt. St. Helens from behind you when you reach the lookout.

Begin by making your way to Carson and heading north on the Wind River Road. You can gas up here.

Once past Stabler, you'll hook a right staying on the Wind River Road and ascend along a great stretch of motorcycle pavement. Just past the snow park, the road will level out and you'll soon turn left onto FS 51, Meadowcreek/Curly Creek Road.

As you drop down Curly Creek Road, watch for signs for McClellan Viewpoint. Turn left into the viewpoint and park. Here there's lot of info about the volcano, a rest room and a great view if the weather is in your favor.

Remount and continue north, making a left out of the parking lot. When you reach FS 90, turn left and proceed toward FS 25. Along the way, you will pass through a small area called Northwoods. Here there's a

26

store, some recreational facilities and sometimes gas (which can be close to two times what you'll find it for at a regular station). Lower-priced fuel is just ahead at the small store in Cougar or in Amboy.

At the T intersection to FS 25, turn left and head to Cougar. The water basins you see to your left are Swift Reservoir and Yale Lake. Just past Yale Lake is Cougar.

West of Cougar is the junction for SR 503. Turn left and make your way south toward Amboy and Yacolt. There are more recreation hollows along the route with small stores and fuel stops if need be. Using the directions provided, we'll skirt downtown Battle Ground and take you along a series of back roads designed to keep you away from the high traffic areas of this growing community. Basket Flat road is a blast!

Eventually you'll head south onto 182nd, do a few little dances (left, right; right, left) and continue south for a while until it becomes Ward Road.

When you see the signs for SR 500 East, follow them and wind through the ells southeast until you reach Dresser Road. Head south there to Blair Road until the road delivers you to the banks of the Washougal River.

At this point, turn left and follow the Washougal river enjoying the scenery as you ride. When you reach the store a few miles east, keep right onto Canyon Road and eventually make a left onto Salmon Falls Road which will take you down to Highway 14. From there you can head east back into The Gorge along the mighty Columbia River.

Saddle time on this ride is about 4 hours. Allow yourself another 1 to 2 hours for stops and lunch.

THREE RIVERS LOOP DIRECTIONS

ODO	Instructions
0.0	Depart Stevenson, WA on SR 14 [NE 2nd St] (East)
3.3	Bear LEFT (North-East) onto Wind River Rd
17.7	Turn RIGHT (North-East) onto Meadow Creek Rd [Wind River Rd]
30.7	Turn LEFT (North-West) onto Curly Creek Rd [Meadow Creek Rd]
32.7	Stop and Enjoy McLellan Lookout
35.4	Turn Left onto FS 90
55.4	Road name changes to SR 503 Spur
63.7	Turn LEFT (South) onto SR 503
72.7	Continue STRAIGHT onto NE Gerber-McKee Rd
74.0	Turn LEFT (South-East) onto NE Amboy Rd
74.2	At Amboy, stay on NE Amboy Rd (South)
77.2	Turn LEFT (East) onto W Yacolt Rd
77.4	Turn RIGHT (South) onto NE Railroad Ave
83.1	Turn LEFT (East) onto NE Hantwick Rd
83.7	Bear RIGHT (West) onto NE Basket Flat Rd
86.0	Turn RIGHT (West) onto NE 280th St (Changes to 279th St)
86.8	Turn LEFT (South) onto NE 182nd Ave
88.3	Turn LEFT (East) onto NE 249th St
88.4	Turn RIGHT (South) onto NE Crawford Rd
88.6	Turn RIGHT to stay on NE Crawford Rd
88.8	Road name changes to NE 182nd Ave
90.4	Turn RIGHT (West) onto NE 209th St
90.7	Turn LEFT (South) onto NE 176th Ave
91.1	Turn LEFT (East) onto NE 199th St, then immediately bear RIGHT
91.5	Bear RIGHT (South) onto NE 182nd Ave
95.4	Road name changes to NE Ward Rd
97.5	Turn LEFT (South-East) onto NE 162nd Ave
98.4	Turn LEFT (East) onto SR 500 [NE Fourth Plain Rd]
105.3	Turn LEFT (East) onto NE 19th St/Dresser Rd
105.8	Road name changes to (NE) Blair Rd
109.2	Turn LEFT (North) onto (SE) Washougal River Rd
116.9	Turn RIGHT (South) onto Canyon Creek Rd
120.0	Bear RIGHT (South-East) onto Salmon Falls Rd
120.5	Turn LEFT (East) onto SR 14
138.4	Arrive Stevenson

Three Rivers

North

Mt. St. Helens

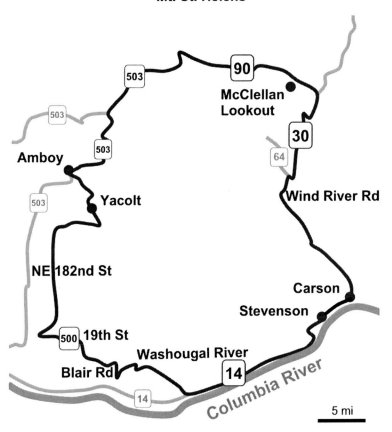

Larch Mountain
DISTANCE: 64 MILES
RIDING TIME: 2 HOURS

Imagine this. You look out from where you are standing and take in a view of not one, not two, but five mountain peaks in the Cascade range. Imagine no more, Larch Mountain is the destination to view this incredible display. This route also spins you around some nice twisties near Corbett and brings you back via the Vista House and Multnomah Falls.

Leaving Stevenson, head west, cross the Bridge of the Gods and ride the super slab to Exit 37. Here you will ride along a section of Hwy 30, the Historic Columbia River Highway and pass a number of waterfalls eventually ascending up to the Vista House.

From there you'll ride west a short stretch and make a 270-degree left turn and ride to Larch Mountain. You'll have the road mostly to yourself for the next 14 miles as there are few residences along the way and not much reason for anyone to be here other than to reach the view that waits at the end.

When you reach the parking area, park near the

Harvey Gilkerson (Sound RIDER!), Scott Renaud (AMA) and David Hough (author Proficient Motorcycling) stand atop Larch Mountain in 2003 with Mt. Hood in the background. Hood is just one of five mountains you'll see from atop the lookout!

trail head, lock up your gear and get ready for a short hike of about a mile. Stay to the right when the trail splits and make your way to the top of the mountain. There they are – Mt. St. Helens, Mt. Rainier, Mt. Adams, Mt. Hood and Mt. Jefferson, all popping their bald heads out of the Cascade Range for your very own viewing pleasure. If you're into panoramic photography, bring along your camera and tripod and fire away.

We like to start this ride in the mid-morning, get to Vista House about 11 and Larch Mountain about noon, finally continuing out west to Troutdale and the Edgefield Hotel for lunch at the Black Rabbit restaurant. Another option is to start a trip into The Gorge from Troutdale, reversing the route.

Vista House is one of the most elegant rest stops on any American roadway. It was masterminded by Sam Hill and Samuel Lancaster as a way to portray the type of road building that was being built in Europe in the early 1900s. The foundation of the structure is built into/around the roadway itself.

LARCH MOUNTAIN DIRECTIONS

ODO	Instructions
0.0	Depart Stevenson on SR 14 [NE 2nd St] (West)
2.6	Turn LEFT (East) onto Bridge of the Gods
3.2	Turn LEFT (South) onto US 30 [Wa-Na-Pa St]
3.4	Take Ramp onto I-84 [US 30]
9.4	At exit 37, turn RIGHT onto Ramp
10.1	Turn LEFT (West) onto NE Tumalt Rd
11.7	Turn RIGHT (West) onto NE Frontage Rd
12.0	Road name changes to US 30 Historic Columbia River Hwy
24.2	Vista House on LEFT
25.1	Turn LEFT (170 Degrees) (East) onto (E) Larch Mountain Rd
33.8	Bear LEFT (North-East) onto (E) Larch Mountain Rd
39.3	Arrive Larch Mountain
39.3	Depart Larch Mountain SOUTH on Larch Mountain Rd
53.6	Bear LEFT (West) onto SE Crown Point Hwy [Historic Columbia River Hwy]
62.3	Keep LEFT onto E Columbia River Hwy
63.2	Keep STRAIGHT onto SW Halsey St
64.0	Arrive Edgefield Hotel

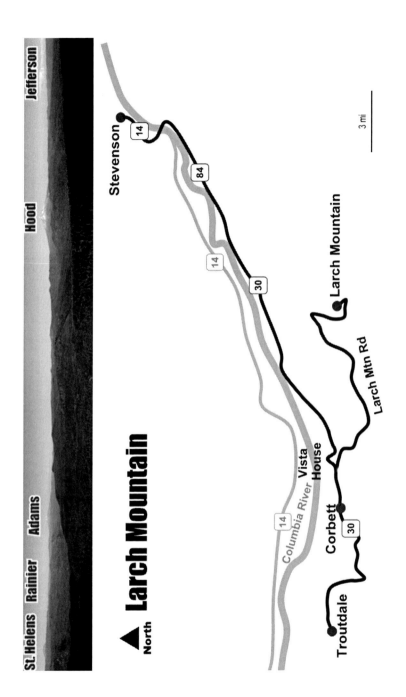

Windy Ridge/Mt. St. Helen's
DISTANCE: 156 MILES ROUND TRIP
RIDING TIME: 5 HOURS

"The guy who engineered this road must have been a motorcyclist," one rider commented to me on a recent ride up this stunning route that takes you out of The Gorge and up to the east side of Mt. St. Helens.

This is a great way to return to Seattle on a ride home from The Gorge. Gas up before you go at Carson. As a loop trip out and back to The Gorge, it's 156 miles, so you'll need to have that much range to make the trip or come up with a fuel alternative. Your alternatives are possible gas availability in North Woods or Cougar, half way on the route. You can also gas up to the north in Randall.

From Carson, ride northwest along the Wind River road and enjoy the meanderings of this great work of art. Upward you climb, twisty after twisty. Make your way to FS 25 until you reach the junction to Windy Ridge. Turn left here and head another 14 miles into the sanctum of Mt. St. Helens where you'll ride through the blast region when the volcano blew its stack in the 80s.

How will you know you've hit the blast region? At

one point you'll round a right hand corner and notice stumps, not trees, and the barren landscape that stretches out to the mountain and beyond. Parking permits or Northwest Forest Passes are required in this area, so if you plan to park for any amount of time, be prepared. Reverse the route to return to The Gorge. If you're heading to Seattle from The Gorge, this makes a great route out.

A word of caution. Forest Road 25 is notorious for eating motorcycles on an almost daily basis every summer. Don't give in to its appetite.

An eerie site in the blast zone: the broken trunk in the foreground as toothpicks of large trees lay across the hillside.

WINDY RIDGE DIRECTIONS

ODO	Instructions
0.0	Depart near Carson on Wind River Rd (East)
14.3	Turn RIGHT (North-East) onto Meadow Creek Rd [Wind River Rd]
27.3	Turn LEFT (North-West) onto Curly Creek Rd [Meadow Creek Rd]
32.1	Road name changes to FS 90
36.6	Turn RIGHT (North-East) onto FS 25
42.1	Turn LEFT to stay on FS 25
61.7	Turn LEFT (West) onto FS 99
78.2	Arrive Windy Ridge

The miner's car is located just past the beginning of the blast zone at the junction of FS 26 on FS 99.

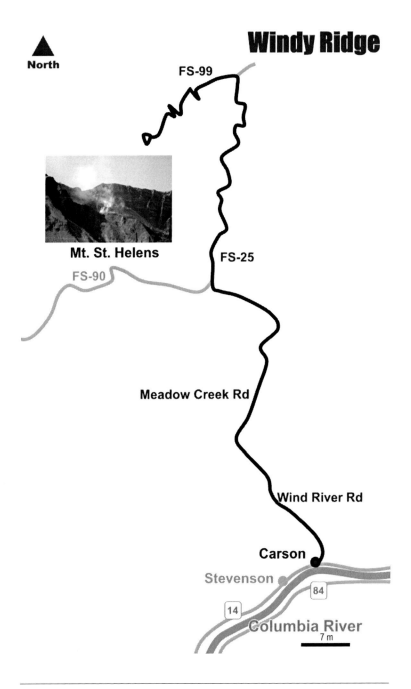

BZ Boogie
DISTANCE: 77 MILES
RIDING TIME: 2.5 HOURS

Up from The Gorge on the Washington side lies the Klickitat Wildlife area and the Yakama Indian Reservation. It's all accessible on pavement and worth the trip if you've got the time. Stunning views of the terrain, a healthy sized look at Mt. Adams and some of the state's finest twisties await your arrival on two wheels.

Begin your ride near Lyle winding your way up the Klickitat River. 23 miles later make a left and head for Glenwood. Along the way you'll see the Klickitat River become a deep carved canyon, so be sure to pull out at the viewpoints for a better look.

Once you leave the canyon, you'll be heading into Glenwood. A stunning view of Mt. Adams beckons you to pull over and break out your camera. The town of Glenwood has little to offer, but there is gas and a store making it a nice rest stop on the route.

The next segment runs the length of the BZ Corner -Glenwood Road and features stunning pavement and road engineering - some of the most fun I think I've ever had in the state. Be sure not to take any of the exits for Appleton unless you're up for a little off-road riding. All roads into Appleton turn to dirt.

Finally you descend from BZ Corner back into The Gorge. Turn around and do it backwards? Perhaps.

BZ BOOGIE DIRECTIONS

ODO	Instructions
0.0	Depart Lyle,on SR 142 (North)
23.5	Turn LEFT (North) onto Glenwood-Goldendale Rd
47.3	Road name changes to E Main St
47.8	Turn LEFT (South) onto S Ash St
47.9	Road name changes to BZ-Glenwood Hwy. Follow through "L" turns
67.4	Turn LEFT (South) onto SR 141
75.2	Keep RIGHT onto SR 141 Alt
77.4	Arrive SR 14

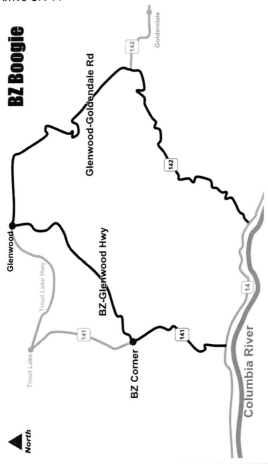

Mt. Adams Runabout
DISTANCE: 164 MILES
RIDING TIME: 4.5 HOURS

Here's a ride that will get you as close as you can get to Mt. Adams on pavement. Half the fun is getting to the stunning view point, the other half is getting back. You see, you could take a straight shot up 141 and be there in no time, but what fun would that be? Instead we've concocted a nice figure eight with plenty of twisties thrown in for good measure. It's a good idea to check the road conditions on the Gifford Pinchot Forest Service Website before travelling to ensure the FS 23, 90 and 88 roads are open.

The ride begins out of Stevenson and heads east to the junction of SR 141 alt, where you'll turn north and make your way to SR 141, again continuing northward. When you arrive at BZ Corner you'll find fuel and snacks if you need em, then take off northeast on the BZ-Glenwood Highway. As discussed in the previous ride, this stretch of road is typically awesome pavement and engineering through the Skamania County section. At the Klickitat county line, the pavement turns to chip seal and a series of ells ensue taking you to Glenwood. Along the way you'll pass through the scenic Conboy Lake National Wildlife Refuge along the Camas Prairie. If it's a nice day you'll also get your first grand view of Mt. Adams.

Once at Glenwood you'll find fuel and refreshments on Main Street at the small market and gas station. Glenwood's kind of laid back and over the years we've not only spotted dogs sleeping right in the middle of the road, but cattle as well.

Continue east out of town following the signs to Trout Lake and the Trout Lake-Glenwood Road. About ten miles from town the road descends and you're faced with a junction. Continue straight and forego the tight lefty. Eventually the road changes names to Little Mountain Road and you'll wind your way into Trout Lake. Here you'll find a few eateries and fuel. This is your last chance for fuel for 55 miles.

Head directly north on Mt. Adams Road (not northwest on SR 141) and follow the signs for Randle. Eventually the road becomes FS23 and you ascend into the forest. The road winds its way around rhythmically and eventually takes you out to a slope with an eastward view of Mt. Adams. There's not much here in terms of an official lookout other than a honey bucket which is usually positioned on the road in the summer months. Take a break, take a few photos and continue.

As you ride along FS 23 you may see a few warning signs for deep dips in the road which we suggest you heed and approach with caution and low speed. Eventually the junction for FS 90 will come up. Continue straight onto FS 90 and proceed for 5 miles. At this point look for the junction with FS 88 and turn left onto it.

At the junction of FS 8851 we have noted a large tractor tire in the middle of the road marking the junction. Bear left and continue along FS 88. As you ride along you may spot a few last glimpses of Mt. Adams through the trees. When you reach Trout Lake, head south down SR 141. On more than one occasion, we have spotted wild turkeys crossing the road between Trout Lake and BZ Corner. Near the high school you will get a final stunning look at Mt. Adams in your rear view mirror. Not a bad view for a high school, huh?

The last section involves hanging a left onto SR 14 and immediately onto the Cook Underwood Road. You will ascend above The Gorge for a while with a few nice pullouts for photo ops. Enjoy the twisties here as you wind your way back to Stevenson.

MT. ADAMS RUNABOUT DIRECTIONS

ODO	Instructions
0.0	Depart Stevenson on SR-14 [NE 2nd St] (East)
19.4	Turn LEFT (North) onto SR-141 Alt
21.6	Turn LEFT (North-West) onto SR-141
29.4	Turn RIGHT (North-East) onto BZ-Glenwood Hwy
49.0	Turn LEFT (West) onto W Main St
49.3	Road name changes to Trout Lake Hwy
58.4	Turn RIGHT (North-West) onto Glenwood Rd
61.9	Road name changes to River Rd
62.6	Turn RIGHT (West) onto Little Mountain Rd
64.4	Turn RIGHT (North) onto SR-141
64.4	At Trout Lake, keep STRAIGHT onto Mt. Adams Rd
65.7	Road name changes to Buck Creek Rd
67.0	Road name changes to FS 23 [Randle Rd]
84.8	Keep STRAIGHT onto FS 90
91.8	Turn LEFT onto FS 88
110.8	Road name changes to Trout Lake Creek Rd
115.0	Turn LEFT (North) onto SR-141
116.7	At Trout Lake, stay on SR-141 (South)
135.7	Keep RIGHT onto SR-141 Alt
137.8	Turn RIGHT (West) onto SR-14
138.0	Turn RIGHT (North) onto Cook-Underwood Rd
147.8	Turn LEFT to stay on Cook-Underwood Rd
152.4	Bear RIGHT (West) onto SR-14
164.6	Arrive Stevenson

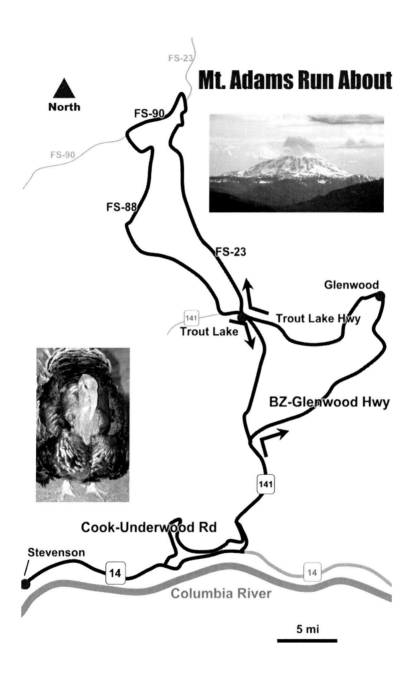

Hood South
DISTANCE: 140 MILES
RIDING TIME: 4 HOURS

Over the years we've come up with a number of ways to get around Mt. Hood. This is a new one for the third edition. If you're going to The Gorge from the Portland/Vancouver Metro area this is a great way to get there.

One could begin with breakfast at the Black Rabbit inside McMenamin's Edgefield Inn. You'd be to the top of Hood in time for lunch at the Lodge or the Ice Axe Grill, then pull into Hood River for a lazy afternoon after a rollicking jaunt down the Cooper Spur Road. Or, if your appetite can make it, skip lunch on the mountain and have a celebratory mid-day meal at Brian's Pourhouse.

Begin by departing Troutdale from the Edgefield heading east along the Old Columbia River Highway. Once in the old town area, turn right and head south down Buxton which will become several other streets and eventually 282nd. Make a left onto Lusted Road, enjoy the country side and work your way along the tasty turns leading down, over and away from the Sandy River. Bear left onto Ten Eyck and follow it to US 26.

Last chance for civilization is here in Gresham. Turn right onto the highway and then left at the sign for SR 211. Follow 211 to the junction with SR 224 and turn left heading south on the Clackamas Highway. As you pass through Estacada you'll be taking a nice forty mile glide alongside the Clackamas River.

Just after you pass the junction for FS 57, you'll reach the junction for FS 42 and turn left heading into the forest lands that lead up to Skyline Drive. Stay on 42/ Skyline for 27 miles to US 26 making a left onto the

44

highway.

At this point you can detour to Government Camp or continue North onto US 35 and taking it toward Hood River.

Float down 35 to the junction for the Cooper Spur road and turn left. Enjoy the twisties here as you work your way toward the west end of the Fruit Loop. At Baseline turn right and follow it left, north, along the Dee Highway which later becomes Tucker Road. One of our favorite tent camping spots is at Tucker County Park along the Hood River. You'll pass it as you ride, so take a moment to investigate or set up camp. Finally you'll wind through some ells into Hood River and descend into town, We end this ride at Brian's Pourhouse because you just don't want to miss having a meal here.

The author's beloved 1988 CB400F/CB1 gawks at the mountain during a lunch break at Timberline Lodge on a sunny summer Sunday afternoon.

HOOD SOUTH DIRECTIONS

ODO	Instructions
0.0	Depart Black Rabbit Restaurant on SW Halsey St (East)
0.8	Keep STRAIGHT onto W Historic Columbia River Hwy
1.0	Turn RIGHT (South) onto S Buxton Ave
1.5	Keep STRAIGHT onto SW Cherry Park Rd
1.5	Road name changes to (S) Troutdale Rd
4.8	Road name changes to SE 282nd Ave
5.1	Turn LEFT (East) onto SE Lusted Rd
14.6	Bear LEFT (East) onto SE Ten Eyck Rd
17.2	Turn LEFT to stay on SE Ten Eyck Rd
19.0	Turn RIGHT (West) onto US 26 [Mt Hood Hwy]
19.2	Turn LEFT (South) onto SR 211 [Meinig Ave]
25.3	Turn LEFT (South) onto SR 211 [SR-224]
30.8	Keep STRAIGHT onto SR 224 [Clackamas Hwy]
55.9	Keep STRAIGHT onto SR 224
70.8	Turn LEFT (South-East) onto FS 42 [Pinhead Creek Rd]
97.0	Turn LEFT (North) onto US 26
107.1	At near Government Camp, stay on SR 35 [Mt Hood Hwy] (South)
121.6	Turn LEFT (West) onto Cooper Spur Rd
132.5	Turn LEFT onto Baseline Dr [Dee Hwy]
132.6	Keep RIGHT onto Dee Hwy [Hood River Hwy]
144.2	Road name changes to Tucker Rd
148.1	Road name changes to 12th St
148.9	Turn LEFT (West) onto May St, then immediately turn RIGHT (North) onto 13th St
149.3	Turn RIGHT (East) onto US 30 [SR 35]
149.7	Arrive Brian's Pourhouse

Hood South

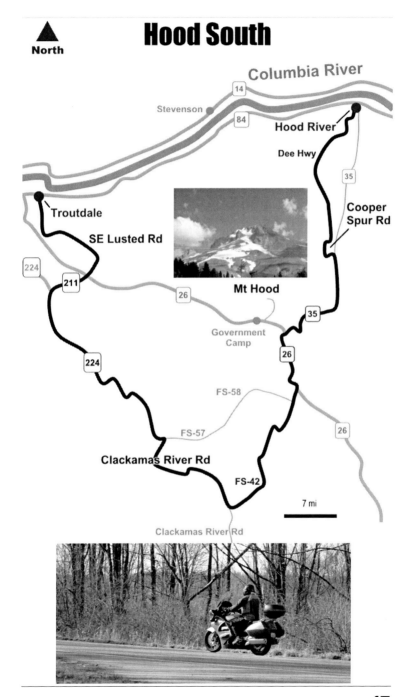

Bluebird Blast
DISTANCE: 166 MILES
RIDING TIME: 4.5 HOURS

This is a nice eastside tour where the landscape is decidedly different from any other ride in this book. Basically it's pretty barren out here, but the road just keeps giving and giving. You'll pass through Bickleton twice so a little history and fuel discussion is in order. First the history.

One of the oldest taverns in Washington State (and they serve food as well) is the Bluebird Inn located in Bickleton. Inside they have one of the oldest Brunswick pool tables dating back to 1884. You can still play on it! So where does the name Bluebird come from? Back in those days, Bluebirds were a common site. Over the years their numbers dwindled until residents built and placed hundreds of bird houses along the roads leading into town. This caused a resurgence in the population and the birds are back. At 3000' above The Gorge, Bickleton used to enjoy full blown winters. Snowmobiles were a viable mode of transportation in the colder months, but today you'll rarely see a snowmobile during winter since the earth has warmed up a bit.

There's no gas in Bickleton ("unless you know the Johnsons" say the locals). Gas up before you ride in Goldendale and again in Mabton.

Our ride begins in Goldendale. Fuel up and find the corner of 3rd and Broadway. Depart bygoing under US 97 and travelling eastward. Although straight for a while, the road will soon start to twist and turn winding in and out of Rock Creek and passing through the Cleveland Burn area. It's great to ride this road in both directions and because of the way we've routed this quasi-in-and-out

48

loop you will. There are plenty of corners you can look right through as you ride here. Bickleton is the first time you can pause for lunch or take a break.

Just past the main town is the junction for East Road. Turn left onto it and make your way through a series of farmland ells and down the Roosevelt Grade to The Gorge below. When you reach SR 14, turn left and take it 15 miles to Alderdale where you once again ascend out of The Gorge into the Horse Heaven Hills. This is wine country here and you'll soon start to see the vast expanse of grapes from every side.

At Glade Road turn left and ride down the grade to Mabton. Here you can fuel up and get a snack. Turn the bike around and reverse your route back up the grade out of Mabton, this time heading directly to Bickleton. Finally complete your ride back to Goldendale.

BLUEBIRD BLAST DIRECTIONS

ODO	Instructions
0.0	Depart Goldendale (East) on E 3rd St [Bickleton Hwy]
0.2	Road name changes to Bickleton Hwy
35.6	Arrive Bickleton
35.8	Turn RIGHT (South) onto East Rd
58.3	Turn LEFT (East) onto SR-14
73.2	Turn LEFT (North) onto Alderdale Rd
86.1	Stay LEFT at Alderdale Rd & McKinley Springs Rd
97.2	Turn RIGHT (North-East) onto Glade Rd
105.0	Arrive Mabton, gas avaliable here
105.2	Depart Mabton on Main St. (South)
126.4	Road name changes to Mabton Hwy
130.3	Road name changes to Goldendale Bickleton Rd
130.8	Arrive Bickleton
130.8	Continue On Goldendale Bickleton Rd (West)
166.4	Arrive Goldendale

Mt, Hood from the route. Look mom, no guardrails!!!

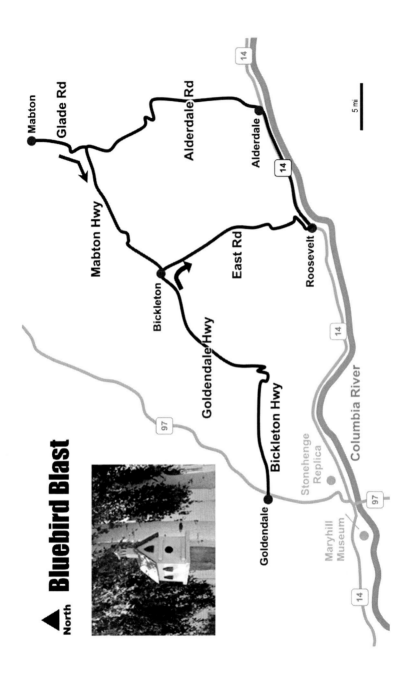

Bluebird Blast

Dualsporting in The Gorge

The Columbia River Gorge is an exceptional area filled with scenic beauty, wildlife and geologic history that is unique and fascinating. With all the volcanic and flood activity that has occurred throughout the region over the last few million years, the area is prime for motorcycling, both on and off road.

The rides in this book are doable on any size dualsport bike including the larger GS type models. Throughout The Gorge you'll discover all kinds of great places to ride, great photo spots.

Adventure, exploring and scenery are all words that describe dualsport motorcycling. As always, ride within your ability, in a safe manner, pay attention to road signs and stay out of closed areas. By adhering to local laws it will provide a better experience for you, the rider, and keep these areas open to riders in the years to come.

A Few Tips

Stabler Country Store

The Country Store at Stabler is a great spot to begin and end several of the rides in Washington state that are included in the dualsport section. The store usually has gas, some cold sandwiches, a light menu and plenty of water and snacks for your ride. The store is located just off Wind River Road north of Carson. To reach Stabler from Stevenson go, east on 14 for 4 miles to the turn-off for Carson, Wind River Road, and continue north for 8.5 miles.

Gas Up

READ THIS! Gas up before you begin a ride. Imagine what can happen if you don't. If gas is not available in Stabler, it will be in Carson.

Ride Within Your Ability

Only ride within your ability. Deep ruts, steep grades, rain, deep gravel, high grass, lightning, low trees or anything else making you think twice about continuing a ride? It's pretty simple—if you got as far as you did, and now you're having second thoughts about continuing in the same direction, turn the bike around and go back.

Never Ride Alone

You've probably heard this one before, but riding your motorcycle off-road in desolate areas is not a great idea. If you don't know anyone at the rally, make some new friends so you have some other people to ride with.

Be Animal Wise

Be aware there is a lot of wildlife throughout this area. It is common to see bear, elk, deer, wolf, coyote and a lot of different birds in the road. When you come upon them, allow them to scatter before you continue with your ride. Never get between a bear and her cub.

Tire Pressure

To better handle a dual sport bike off-road, a lot of riders tend to drop their air pressure below what the manufacturer recommends. Manufacturer-recommended air pressure levels are typically based on what is suitable for pavement riding. Once you're off-road, a slightly lower air pressure can be advantageous for better handling. Consult your operator's manual for details.

We've found that a 15% reduction in air pressure from the recommended levels helps handling considerably. Your results may vary. Many riders drop their air pressure when they reach the dirt and raise it again for pavement at the end of the ride.

Single Track Areas

Being that this book was created to accommodate all sizes, makes and models of modern-day dualsport bikes, you will not find any specific single track rides here. There are two single track areas near Stevenson; Jones ORV Park in Washougal and an area along the Cispus River in the Blue Lake area between Randle and Trout Lake.

Existing Roads

At the time of publication, we had pre-ridden all the roads indicated on the maps contained in this book and verified they actually existed and were in rideable condition. The best digital references we had for maps came from software utilizing USGS data. The roads we've marked exist; the other roads you see on the maps may or may not exist. If you decide to go exploring, do so with extreme caution and never ride beyond your ability.

For all you explorers - if you head down a road and notice the weeds in the middle getting taller, like 15" high, or the trees growing right into you with vegetation slapping at your hands - then we can almost assure you the next sign will be ruts and likely impassable washed-out conditions. It's time to turn around. Don't wait until the conditions become so gnarly that you can't turn your bike around, do it sooner rather than later.

With Mt. Hood in the distance, gravel roads like this provide views that can't be had from pavement.

Map Information and Estimated Distances (ODO)

On the maps, rides have directions with turn-by-turn information noted on the left. These are estimates based on our GPS pre-routing. Your odometer readings may vary slightly based on accuracy.

The maps in this book are just the tip of the iceberg. Consider picking up a Benchmark atlas from the Sound *RIDER!* online store for more info. There are many great roads in this area, so get out there and ride!

Hey Kids—It's Fire Season

All you have to do is watch the news for a few minutes each night and all you hear from June to September is the fire here and the fire there. While it's a pleasure, it's also a privilege for you to be able to travel these roads during this time of year. Respect the beauty of the forest in brown, blue and green, not red.

THE RIDES

Cougar Rock
Rating: **Easy**
Distance: **33.5 miles**

This short trip to Cougar Rock is an easy one and a great way to get a taste of the Gifford Pinchot National Forest.

The ride begins out of Stabler and proceeds west to where you'll turn right at the local forestry office onto FS 43. Follow the road a few miles and it eventually turns to gravel. At this point you'll make a steep ascent up a 16% grade until you finally reach the junction to FS 41, where you will turn right. Although your GPS may not say so, FS 43 does go through to FS 41. The connecting section was built more recently after the eastern section of FS 41 was terminated following the end of a logging operation.

Making your way west on FS 41, you'll begin to see Mt. Hood on your left - and if it's clear enough, a peak-a-boo view of Mt. Jefferson further to the south. When you arrive at the junction of FS 4220, turn right and follow it along the burn area. Keep your eyes peeled for a view of Mt. St. Helens along here. A little later you'll be treated to a view of Mt. Adams to the Northeast. That's a lot of mountain views in a single day! Soon, out in front of you, will be Cougar Rock.

Cougar Rock appears at the junction of FS 4220 and makes for a great background if you're looking to get some shots of you with your bike, or perhaps friends along on your ride. To return to Stabler, take FS 42 to the right and proceed eastward down the hill. The road dumps you out on FS 54 and you continue easterly. Eventually that road becomes Little Soda Springs, then becomes Szydlo Road. and you continue south back into Stabler, making a left on Hemlock Road to get back to the main road that will return you towards Carson and Stevenson via the Wind River Road.

COUGAR ROCK DIRECTIONS

ODO	Instruction
0	From Wind River Rd at Stabler, turn left onto Hemlock Rd
1.4	Turn right onto FS 43
14.0	Turn right onto FS 41 and drive west
16.8	Turn right onto FS 4220
19.6	Keep right onto FS 42 and drive NE
27.4	Continue straight onto FS 54 and drive east, then southeast
33.5	Arrive Stabler

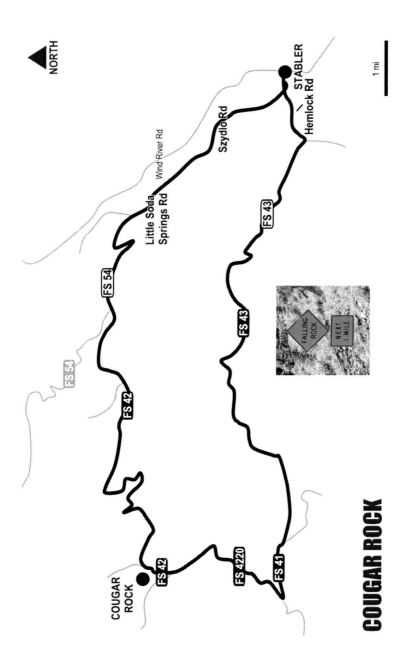

Sunset Falls
Rating: Easy
Distance: 58.3 miles

Here's a nice loop that makes for a great ride to sandwich a lunch into. Be sure to gas up before you ride.

From Stabler you'll follow the same set of directions as the beginning of the Cougar Rock ride. West on Hemlock Road, right at the forestry office onto FS 43, up the 16% grade to FS 41, right and now straight across the ridge toward Lookout Mountain.

For those with a desire for views, you can take a side trip up the road to Lookout Mountain, although the spur road is a bit squirrelly. If you decide not to take it, there's still another viewpoint just down the road from there that is very nice just before the road descends toward Sunset Campground. Look for the dirt cul-de-sac as a landmark for this viewpoint. It's marked on your map as "The Other Lookout."

When you descend into Sunset Campground, you'll see the falls on your right just before you cross the bridge onto FS 42. You can eat lunch here, or head east up the road a mile or so to another fall and have lunch there. From here, wind your way through a series of Forest Service roads that will lead you towards the lava flow at Trout Creek on FS 34. Eventually you'll pop out on FS 54, a fun single lane, paved twisty used by loggers. Wind your way back to civilization into the Stabler area.

SUNSET FALLS DIRECTIONS

ODO	Instruction
0.0	Get on Hemlock Rd and drive west
1.2	Turn right onto FS 417
10.0	Get on Sunset Hemlock Rd and drive west
24.8	Arrive Sunset Falls Area
24.9	Turn right onto FS 42
28.1	Keep left onto FS 4211
31.4	Turn right onto FS 53
32.8	Continue left on FS 38 and drive north
39.3	Turn right onto FS 37
46.7	Continue lefton FS 34 and drive northeast
49.5	Turn right onto FS 54
58.8	Road becomes Little Soda Springs Rd
62.1	Turn left onto Hemlock Rd
62.4	Arrive Stabler

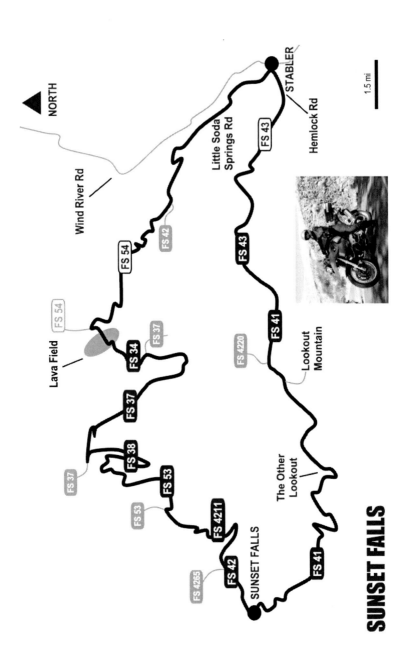

SUNSET FALLS

Trapper Creek
Rating: Easy
Distance: 60.5 miles

Here's a ride that incorporates some of the finest pavement and gravel combinations you'll find in the Gifford Pinchot National Forest.

The ride begins in Stabler, refresh your water and snacks and we'll be on our way.

Begin by heading west on Hemlock Road, then making a right onto Szydlo Road, which then becomes Little Soda Springs. At the Y, keep left and ride onto FS 54. Get ready for some pavement fun as you wind and twist your way up one of the most magically-engineered roads ever to be built in a national forest.

After about 10 miles, the road becomes gravel and you ascend a bit more and then descend into Canyon Creek. The road turns to pavement again and that's your signal that the junction for FS 57 is near. Turn right onto FS 57 and make your way up the pavement. The road makes a hard right and becomes FS 5704. Do not continue straight onto the unpaved portion of FS 57 as it's a two-track road to nowhere and becomes dangerous after about a mile.

Soon FS 5704 becomes gravel again and you continue a northeasterly ride past sister rocks with views of St. Helen's and later Mt. Adams. Merge onto FS 58 and follow it around keeping right as it eventually becomes FS 60. When you hit pavement, you're on Soiuxon Road and heading south where you meet up with Wind River Road. Turn right to get back down to Stabler and Carson.

TRAPPER CREEK DIRECTIONS

ODO	Instruction
0	From Wind River Rd get on Hemlock Rd and drive west
0.5	Turn right onto Szydlo Rd
4.0	Keep left onto FS 54
6.7	Turn right onto FS 54
28.5	Turn right onto FS 57
32.1	Turn right onto FS 5704 and drive south
36.3	Merge onto on FS 58 and drive northeast
46.6	Merge onto FS 64 and drive east
52.7	Merge right onto Wind River Rd
60.5	Arrive Stabler

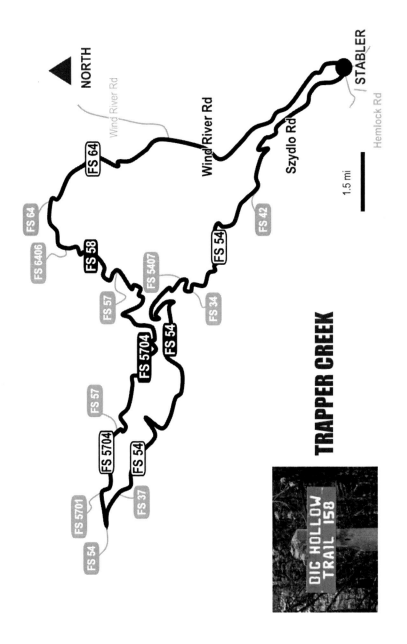

Three Corner Rock
Rating: Moderate
Distance: 32 miles

Here's a nifty ride with views through the Yacolt Burn State Forest that will take you high above Table Mountain (which is visible from the fairgrounds to the Northwest).

For starters, the State Forest roads (County Grades or CGs) are maintained with a slightly larger grade of crush gravel and they can be a bit more squirrelly than those maintained by the US Forest Service. Tire pressure is critical to making this more controllable. See the section on that in the front of your map pack.

The ride begins just below Skamania Lodge on Red Bluff road. As you continue on the road it will turn to gravel and become CG 2000. Look for the waterfall at the bridge.

The Northwest corner. You can park at the bottom and climb to the top. Photo by RJ Myrup (rjs-s.com)

Next you're climbing up into the state forest. What begins as a northwest ascent eventually does a ninety degree turn and you are heading southward toward your destination of Three Corner Rock. Just after the apex, the road changes to CG 1440 and then CG 1408. Eventually the junction for CG 1400 comes up on your left; turn left. Continue to the left where the road becomes CG 1500A which you will use to get to your destination, Three Corner Rock at 3550 feet. From here there are views of Helens, Rainier, Adams, Hood and Jefferson. This once was a fire lookout. Not a bad place to have spent days monitoring the land.

Once you've had a look around, retrace your steps back down the hill and turn left onto CG 1400 at the junction with CG 1408. Continue straight southward.

When the road becomes paved, you are on Kueffler Road which will bring you back into The Gorge at Highway 14. Just across the street is Beacon Rock which is a great hiking spot with a view. It takes about 60 minutes to hike up and back down.

THREE CORNER ROCK DIRECTIONS

ODO	Instruction
0	Get on Rock Creek Dr and drive southwest
0.3	Turn right onto Foster Creek Rd
1.2	Turn left onto CG 2000 (Red Bluff Rd)
9.2	Stay left onto CG 1440 and drive southwest (becomes CG 1408)
16.3	Turn left onto CG 1400 and drive northeast
20.5	Stay left onto CG 1500 and drive northwest
22.1	Return to CG 1408
24.7	Turn left onto CG 1408
25.0	Turn left onto CG 1420 and drive east/south
29.6	Turn left onto CG 1408 and drive south
32.7	Arrive Hwy14 & Beacon Rock

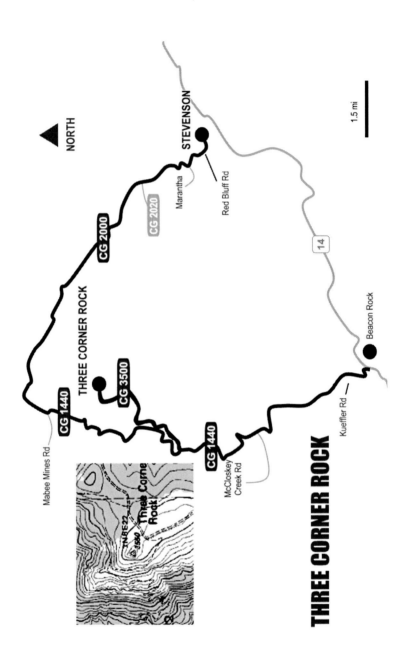

THREE CORNER ROCK

Timberline East
RATING: EASY
DISTANCE: 55 MILES

Timberline Lodge makes a great lunch destination. You can dine in the formal dining room, or hide out at the cafe bar upstairs. Windows peer out from all directions: to the north there's majestic Mt. Hood, to the south there's the national forest below and, on a clear day, glimpses of other peaks.

How you get there is another story. We have several pavement options in this book and with the new edition we're pleased to offer two dualsport options as well. Both rides depart from Hood River.

Sharing the road with mountain bikers on FS 17

For this version, the Timberline East ride we begin at the junction of US 35 and head east up the old Columbia River Highway. Once at the top we go right onto Highline and left onto East Side Road. Take a moment to stop at Panorama Point for a stunning look across to Mt. Hood. Continue south on East Side Road and make a left onto Fir Mountain Grade. Follow it south as it turns into gravel and takes you into the forest. Eventually the road junctions with FS 17 where you'll continue your southerly direction. At the junction of FS 44, ride west out to US 35. Then turn left, follow the junction for US 26 toward Portland and in a few miles hang a right up to Timberline Lodge. Consider using the Timberline West route to get back to Hood River.

TIMBERLINE EAST DIRECTIONS

ODO	Instruction
0.0	At US 35 get on Old Columbia River Dr and drive east
0.7	Turn right onto Highline Rd
4.8	Turn left onto Eastside Rd
5.6	Turn right onto Fir Mountain Rd
25.4	Turn left onto FS 17
27.6	Turn right onto FS 44 Dufur Mill Rd
35.3	Turn left onto Hwy 35
48.2	Take the US 26 W ramp to the right towards Portland
50.8	Turn right onto Timberline Hwy
54.8	Arrive Timberline Lodge

Timberline East

NORTH

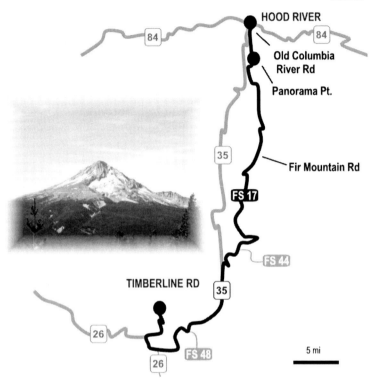

It's not uncommon to come across hunters in the forest, especially in the late summer and early fall months. Riding without antlers on your helmet is advised.

71

Timberline West
RATING: MODERATE
DISTANCE: 67 MILES

The east route up to Timberline is a little easier than the west route, but even this route can be done with a full-size adventure bike.

We begin on the west end of Hood River at the corner of Cascade Avenue and Country Club Road. Head west on Country Club Road. At the intersection for Post Canyon, turn right and continue on. Eventually the road turns to gravel, Work your way up the slopes turning right onto Riordan Hill Drive where you'll pass two water retention basins on your right as you enter the Kingsley Park area. Continue southwest turning right onto Larch Mountain Road and left onto Dead Point Road.

From here you wind your way back down the grade with great views of Hood along the way. At the bottom you are spilled onto Punchbowl Road which you'll follow south and stay right as it becomes Lost Lake Road and follow the pavement up to the junction with FS 18. Turn left and wind your way up the gravel through the Lolo Pass area.

At the top of the pass, turn left continuing onto the pavement and making your way toward US 26. Turn left onto the main highway and proceed past Government Camp (fuel here if you need it) and turn left onto Timberline Road following the sign up to the lodge.

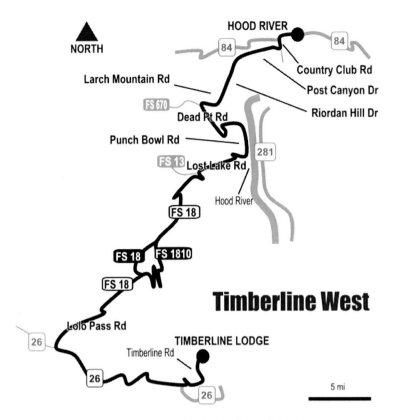

TIMBERLINE WEST DIRECTIONS

ODO	Instruction
0.0	Get on Country Club Rd and drive southwest
1.8	Turn right onto Post Canyon Dr
6.3	Turn right onto Riordan Hill Dr
7.8	Turn right onto Larchmountain Rd
12.6	Turn left onto Dead Point Rd
20.6	Get on Punch Bowl Rd and drive southeast
20.7	Keep right onto Lost Lake Rd
21.0	Turn left onto FS 18 Lolo Pass Rd
48.8	Turn left onto US 26
62.0	Turn left onto Timberline Road
67.6	Arrive Timberline Lodge

Lava Love
Rating: Moderate
Distance: 106 miles

Come on in – the lava's fine! Well at least since it cooled down so long ago. In fact, so long ago that the forest has grown up around it and it's not too obvious from riding here that this area was a pyroclastic playground back when Mt. Adams was spewing.

But today there are many fine roads and you still have the chance to experience the terrain and learn about the evolution of the area. On the south there is a spur road that will take you in for a panoramic view of the lava bed area. To the north, there is a system of lava tubes and ice caves you can venture into (watch for the signs).

The loop we provide here is just a part of the system of roads in the area. If you explore beyond the route, use caution on the various side roads.

Begin the loop from Stabler and head south to Panther Creek Road which becomes FS 65. Go right onto FS 68 and follow along the south side of the big lava bed. A left on FS 66 will take you to a left onto FS 6605 which will take you up the spur for an overview of the Big Lava Bed. Return to FS 66 and head north. You are now riding along an ancient lava bed. Notice the trees on the left in the bed only grow to a max of about 100 feet, then die looking like large matchsticks. This is because pumice is always about 15

degrees colder than regular ground and eventually freezes the tree roots. After you pass the wetland area, turn right onto FS 60 where you'll turn right and ride onto SR 141. Head into Trout Lake for gas and snacks or lunch at the Bear Creek Cafe.

To complete the route, backtrack on Road 141 and head west across the lava tube area onto FS 60. You can explore the marked areas and eventually make your way back into Stabler using FS 60, left when you get to Wind River Road. A little trivia – some of the lava tubes are cold enough inside for ice and were tested for food refrigeration by the Forest Service in the 1920s. Keep your eyes peeled for century old potatoes, cheeses and dried fruits! Also during pre-routing, this is the area where a rare grey wolf sighting occurred.

LAVA LOVE DIRECTIONS

ODO	Instructions
0.0	Get on Wind River Rd and ride south
2.7	Turn left onto Old State Rd
2.9	Turn left onto Panther Creek Rd
7.6	Turn right onto FS 68 (6800)
29.5	Turn left onto FS 66
30.6	Keep left onto Big Huckleberry Rd
39.6	Turn left onto FS 6605
51.3	Turn left onto FS 66 and ride north
64.7	Turn right onto FS 60 (Carson Guler Rd)
72.7	Turn right onto Hwy 141
74.0	Arrive Bear Creek Café
74.0	Get on Hwy 141 and drive northwest
83.3	Turn left onto FS 60 (Carson Guler Rd)
83.6	Ice cave area
105.0	Turn left onto Wind River Rd
106.0	Arrive Stabler

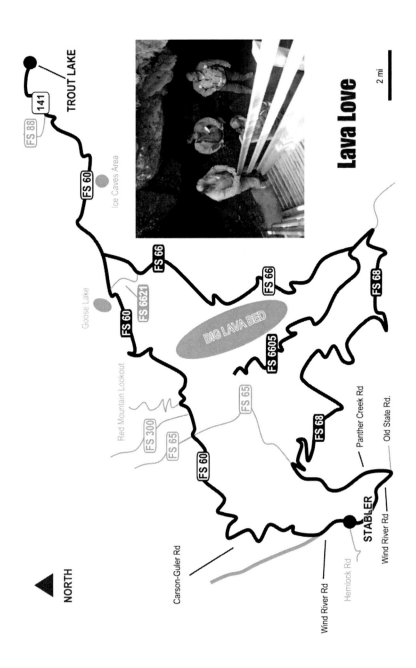

Lava Love

76

Old Dalles Road
RATING: EASY
DISTANCE: 35 MILES

Prior to the advent of US 30, there was only one way to get between The Dalles and Hood River. That was using the Old Dalles Road. Much of the old road still exists today. As you ride imagine, yourself in a wagon train making your way between the two cities. On a bike it only takes a little over an hour, but back in the old wagon days it was more like a day.

This makes a nice morning ride into The Dalles from Hood River and then you can take a leisurely ride on Skyline road to reach the Mt. Hood area.

The ride begins in Hood River at the junction of Highway 35 and Old Columbia River Drive. Ride up the grade and proceed south on Highline, turn left on Eastside Road and take a gander at Panorama Point if you feel the urge. Then continue south down Eastside Road and turn left onto Old Dalles Drive. Ride two miles and follow the road to the right, south as it turns into gravel.

The roads are fairly well signed out here so locating Wilson and Huskey are a breeze. Make a right onto Mosier Creek and take a short ride to Digger Road and ride up the grade. At the top, turn right onto Carroll which becomes Vensel, then hang a left on Chenoweth Creek and descend. At the bottom hang a right onto Browns Creek which will wind around and become Cherry Heights. The ride ends at 10th and Cherry Heights in the Dalles.

OLD DALLES ROAD DIRECTIONS

ODO	Instructions
0.0	Get on Old Columbia River Dr and drive east
0.7	Turn right onto Highline Rd
0.9	Turn left onto Eastside Rd
2.8	Turn left onto Old Dalles Dr
4.8	Turn right onto Elder Rd
7.3	Keep left onto Old Dalles Dr
8.3	Turn left onto Old Dalles Dr
11.0	Turn right onto Huskey Rd
11.4	Turn right onto Wilson Rd
15.1	Turn right onto Mosier Creek Rd
16.4	Turn left onto Digger Rd
17.4	Turn right onto Carroll Rd [becomes Vensel Rd]
21.4	Turn left onto Chenoweth Creek Rd
25.7	Turn right onto Browns Creek Rd
29.8	Follow road 180, becomes Cherry Heights Rd
35.2	Arrive Downtown The Dalles

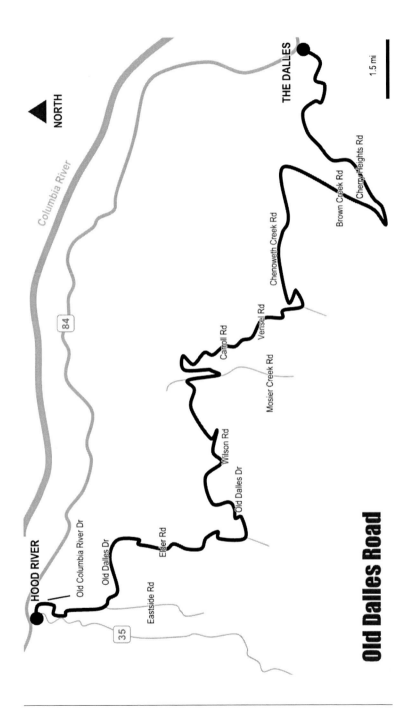

Indian Heaven
RATING: EASY
DISTANCE: 29 MILES

Looking for a scenic way home from The Gorge? If you're heading toward Seattle this is a nice gravel alternate to the pavement of the Wind River Road (which isn't too bad itself).

The Native Americans used to breed horses for the Yakima Nation here in the Indian Heaven wilderness. In fact, there's an old abandoned horse track around these parts. Today there are several modern day horse camps, so keep your eyes out for trucks with trailers.

You begin by leaving Carson and heading north on the Wind River road turning right onto Old State Road. Almost immediately turn left onto Panther Creek and follow the road through the woods north. Past the four way with the gravel Carson/Guler Road (FS 60), the road will become FS 65, turn to gravel and shortly you'll stumble into the Falls Creek Horse Camp.

Proceed north and eventually the road will meet with FS 30. Turn left and follow it to the Curly Creek road where you'll make a right and head down to the end of the ride at the spectacular McClellan Viewpoint.

INDIAN HEAVEN DIRECTIONS

ODO	Instructions
0.0	Begin on Old State Road at the junction of Wind River Road
90.1	Turn left on Panther Creek Rd and ride north
11.2	Road turn to gravel
22.7	Turn left onto FS 30
27.1	Turn right onto Curly Creek Rd
29.3	Arrive McClellan Viewpoint

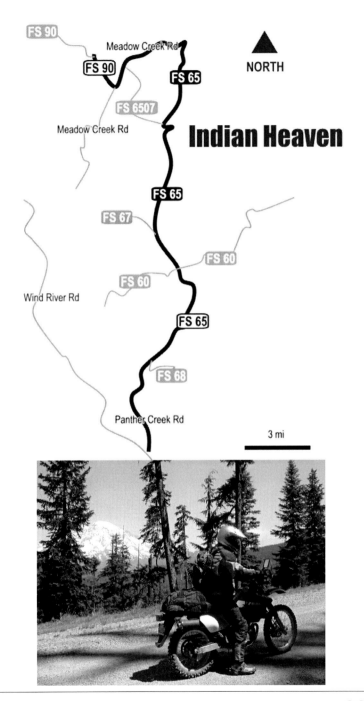

3 Rivers Dualsport Loop
RATING: EASY
DISTANCE: 112 MILES

We began a few years ago with a 3 Rivers pavement ride. The concept was to route people along the Columbia, Wind and Washougal rivers for a day ride loaded with scenery. After a few years it became obvious one could create a dualsport version of the same ride. In fact, we've run simultaneous poker runs using both routes and the same checkpoints along the way.

For our dualsport version, you depart Stevenson heading west on SR 14 following the Columbia River as it flows west toward Portland. When you reach Salmon Falls, turn right and make a left at the top of the hill on Canyon Creek. Ride until you reach the Washougal store and turn right proceeding along the river. When you cross the bridge at the end of the pavement, go left and follow the L 1200 road northwest to the paved Dole Valley Road. Ride north up Dole Valley and keep left onto Sunset Falls. At Railroad Avenue, turn right and continue northwest to Yacolt. At Yacolt, turn right onto Amboy Road and ride to Amboy.

At Amboy you can find food and fuel. Nick's Bar & Grill does the trick if you want a meal.

Depart Amboy heading north, then east on SR 503. Just a jog down the road, turn right on Healy and go eastward across the Chelatchie Prairie. When the road Y's go right and continue on FS 54 all the way back to the Stabler area where it turns into Little Soda Springs. Turn left on Hemlock and park your bike just before the bridge that crosses over the Wind River. Walk onto the bridge and notice that the river is actually winding its way through a broken lava tube. Depart the area south on the Wind River Road and return to The Gorge.

3 RIVERS DUALSPORT LOOP DIRECTIONS

ODO	Instructions
0.0	Depart Stevenson heading West on SR 14
17.8	Turn right onto Salmon Falls Rd
18.4	Turn left onto Canyon Creek Rd
21.5	Turn right onto Washougal River Rd
32.7	Turn left onto 1200 Rd
48.4	Turn right onto NE Dole Valley Rd
53.5	Turn left onto NE Sunset Falls Rd
55.5	Turn right onto NE Railroad Ave
58.1	Turn left onto W Yacolt Rd
58.2	Turn right onto N Amboy Ave
61.4	Turn right onto NE Gerber-McKee Rd
62.8	At Amboy get on Hwy 503 and drive northeast
65.3	Turn right onto NE Healy Rd
74.3	Follow road right onto FS 54 and drive east
100.0	Turn left onto Hemlock Rd
100.0	Arrive Stabler
109.1	Keep right onto SR 14
112.2	Arrive Stevenson

Dualsport camping in The Gorge at sunrise.

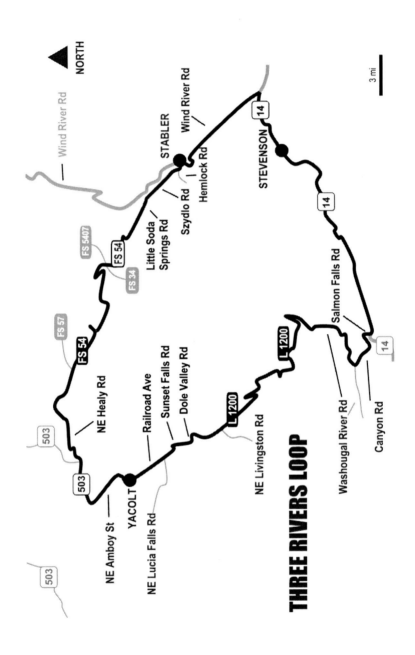

Commonsense riding practices...

For riding in The Gorge or anywhere else for that matter

Having ridden in and out of The Gorge extensively since 2000, I've seen my fair share of crashes. Enough so that I have plenty of statistics logged on circumstances involving many of the crashes. Having run a rally in The Gorge since 2003, I get to write up about a half dozen injury crash reports each year which must be sent back to the American Motorcyclist Association for insurance purposes. Not one of my favorite jobs, but it's a telling tale.

We now have hundreds of photographs of people riding motorcycles in The Gorge. They are also a telling tale. The pictures provide us a chance to look at how people are riding, what they're doing correctly and what they're doing wrong. No doubt they're going to ride the same way whether they're in The Gorge or somewhere else.

So I couldn't get into writing the third edition of this book without touching on the subject of rider safety and skills. During our rally each year we experience about a 3% crash rate, with about half those resulting in injuries. The most common are low sides and high sides due to overriding one's abilities, T-bones typically involving cagers, group crashes due to riding too closely and failed quick stops in general. There will always be crashes, but the more we can do to reduce them the better it is for everyone.

Through a basic motorcycle safety class provided by all States we learn…the basics. And in some cases that

85

keeps us out of trouble on the road. In others it does not, as we'll soon see. Skills authors and advanced riding instructors like Keith Code, David Hough, Lee Parks, Reg Pridmore, Doc Wong and Freddy Spencer teach advanced skills you can't get from a State-run course. Digging in deeper and constantly honing your skills will make you a better rider and more prepared for potential circumstances before they happen. What I'm going to cover here are some techniques they teach as well as a few I've come up with on my own for dealing with the twisties and groups of riders.

RIDE WITH A PLAN

Before I get started, I have a little motto to take with you each time you ride. This one comes from my friend Bruce Scott, who got it from Freddy Spencer, who got it from…well, who knows? The motto is "RIDE WITH A PLAN!" Remember it every time you ride.

I'm going to cover about a dozen things in this chapter and like any motorcycle instruction book or class it's just not possible to ride away and work on each point all at the same time. So take one thing from this chapter and focus on it next time you ride. When you've mastered it and it becomes second nature to you, move onto the next tip and work on it. I sometimes spend a few weeks just working on one element of my riding. All of a sudden you realize you're doing it without thinking about it and an ear-to-ear grin ensues.

RIDING BEYOND YOUR ABILITY

Are there times you scare the hell out of yourself by riding over the center line when you didn't mean to, stopping too short or you feel the bike starting to slide out from under you? You are riding beyond your ability.

We've all done it.

Your bike is capable of doing the things you want it to do, but you may be lacking the technique required to get through a turn without having a heart attack, make a quick stop or avoid an obstacle when it appears. If you're having these experiences with regularity, it's time to figure out why these things are happening and what you can do to curb such circumstances. Every time you don't do something about it you're one step closer to your next crash and you may be endangering other riders around you as well.

Have you taken a basic riding skills class? If you answered 'no,' sign up for one sooner rather than later. If you answered 'yes,' ask yourself the next question – 'Have I taken an intermediate riding skills class and do I take one about every two years to brush up on skills I may be letting slide?' If you answered 'no,' sign up for one and get an instructor's point of view on where you can improve your skills. If you answered 'yes,' then ask yourself – 'Do I read riding skills books, take additional classes such as instructional track days and other classes offered in my area. If you answered 'no,' it's time to move your skills to the next level through the various educational opportunities available to you.

Whatever your skills level and wherever you plan to take yourself next, it's important to remember one thing. If you get a notion that you are over-riding your abilities, it's time to slow down, relax and work more on your technique.

TECHNIQUE BEFORE SPEED

Take the three words above and let's reverse them. Speed before technique. Ouch. That's a recipe for a crash right there and it's one of the most common reasons why people crash.

Everyone can go fast but not everyone has the technique to enter a corner without grabbing a handful of brakes along the way and getting into a high side or low side incident. Work on your technique at slower speeds and before you know it, your comfort level will increase and you'll start seeing higher numbers on the speedometer as you leave turns.

I'm not endorsing any sort of high speed antics here, mind you. With the right bike, the twisties along a State Route like Washington's Highway 14 are quite fun even at the legal speed limit. And yet we've seen numerous crashes where riders were too hot for their own abilities in turns. They had not developed basic skill sets to handle simple cornering maneuvers.

Using 'technique before speed' as a guideline, I find cornering much more exhilarating, safer and, overall, much more fun.

NEVER RIDE FASTER THAN YOU CAN STOP

Never ride faster than you can stop. The concept seems to make sense. But have you ever recited the statement... at 60 mph in a blind turn? Try it and you'll see what I mean.

There are going to be times in your motorcycle riding history when you'll need to make a quick stop, avoid the unexpected and make it through the situation hopefully without crashing. If you can do that at any point during your ride, then you're probably having more fun riding your motorcycle and doing it more safely than others around you who may be having a tough time.

For one of my 'ride with a plan' exercises, I ask myself the question 'am I riding faster than I can stop?' whenever I think of it. It seems to naturally come to mind when I notice I've overridden a turn so I slow down for awhile and focus on the question for the next few miles of

88

twisties. At that point, I fall back into the 'technique before speed' scenario and begin enjoying the ride again. The smile returns to my face and I've had a better ride for it.

ELBOWS BENT, DOWN AND RELAXED

So let's get into a technique at this point. Have you ever gone into a corner, felt like you were having to work to keep the bike on track and feeling a bit overwhelmed coming out the other side rather than exhilarated? I was having this issue so I had an instructor watch me ride and it all became clear. I was extending my arms in turns rather than leaning forward bending my elbows. David Hough calls this 'riding with your shoulders' because essentially all the pressure and commands to the handle bars are emanating from your shoulders, rather than your wrists and hands, leading to less control and less confidence as a result.

Bending the elbows in the turns will transfer all the work of controlling the bike to the wrists and hands which is right next to where the action is anyhow – in the handle bars.

On some bikes, bent elbows are often a natural occurrence, such as on a Goldwing, a cruiser or maxi scooter. On a sportbike or sport touring bike it's less likely the ergonomic norm. Sit on your motorcycle upright with your spine straight up and down and see if your elbows are bent or fully extended.

If they are fully extended you have two choices. You can lean forward to get them bent in the turns, or you can add a set of bar risers to the bike to get the handle bars where they need to be so you always have a bend in your elbows while sitting upright. You're looking for about a fifteen-degree bend here.

The next question is where are your elbows when

you have them bent in a turn? The correct position would be down which will once again allow the wrist and hands to manage control of the bike. If they are up, say at shoulder level, that will tend to lock your wrists.

Finally it's time to do the flapping test. As you ride through a turn you should have your elbows bent, down and so relaxed that you can flap them a bit like a bird. This would be your final check to know that the wrists and hands are in control.

Getting these elbows down will greatly enhance the riders confidence in the corner. Photo by RJ Myrup (rjs-s.com)

FIXATION AND INATTENTIVENESS

Fixation is what happens when you're riding along in a group and you realize you've been spending copious amounts of your riding time looking at the brake light and license plate of the rider in front of you…instead of noticing that 15 mph warning sign…you just passed…too late…you just crashed.

Whether you're in a group ride or just following a four-wheel vehicle in front of you it's easy to get fixated and it's one of the top reasons people crash. They lose sight of what's going on around them, miss important warning signs and the next thing they know there's a tow truck driver on the scene pulling their bike from a ditch with a cable winch.

Keep your head up and constantly scan ahead and around you as you ride.

Inattentiveness occurs when the road hasn't changed much in a while such as riding on an interstate or slabbing on a straight section of a State highway. It's one of the most common crash reasons listed on State crash records. Staying alert can mean the difference between avoiding a T-Bone collision with a left-turning car or going to the hospital.

We all have those moments when several miles of road goes by and we have no recollection of the scenery we just passed through. If this happens it may be a signal that it's time to stop, take a break, have a little hydration and snack and start anew on your journey.

PEER PRESSURE TO KEEP UP

Are there times when you feel like there are a number of riders in your group who can outride you but you need to keep up with them no matter what? Either they or you are creating a bit of pressure on you and it's time to take stock in the situation and end it.

Never feel like you have to keep up with riders who ride better or faster than you. If you need to, drop back to the back of the group and let them go ride their own ride while you ride yours at your own pace and ability.

If you plan to ride in the back, it's a good idea to have an understanding of the route and stopping points before you leave. That way you won't have to stay up with the group to know where to go next.

This is a prime example near Mt. St. Helens of what can occur if you fixate on the rider in front of you. While the rider in front completed the turn, this bike and its rider did not focusing on the rider in front, rather than the 15 m.p.h. sign.

SMALL PODS RATHER THAN LARGE GROUPS

One day during our rally, we had scheduled a group ride to Larch Mountain in Oregon. Forty people arrived and were supposed to follow the ride leader. The first challenge was getting forty motorcyclists over the Bridge of the Gods through the toll booth on the Oregon side. Sitting on the Bridge of the Gods isn't such a bad deal… until you look down. Through the grated bridge you can watch the Columbia River moving swiftly forty feet below. Not so fun if you're not fond of heights. The ride leader got the group to the final road and let the group sort it as to who was going to go first, second and so on. Inevitably friends want to stay together and before you know it you've got a lesser-skilled rider sandwiched between a half dozen better-skilled riders in front and behind. Passing antics ensue, fixation occurs and before you know it someone goes down. This is nothing new in the world of motorcycling and it often ends with several riders going down trying to avoid the accident ahead.

Today during the rally we offer maps for suggested rides and encourage like-skilled riders to ride together in small pods of six or less. There's no specific departure time and we want everyone to ride at their own pace, not someone else's. By moving to this format we have managed to cut our accident percentages in half.

You can do the same thing with your own group whenever and wherever you ride.

But here's another added benefit to this format. Food establishments loathe it when a dozen or more motorcyclists enter the doorway all at once. Space the pods out by five-to-ten minutes with the faster group in front. When the first pod arrives it allows them time to get seated and put their order in before the next pod arrives. As a result, you'll be better received by the wait staff and cooks when it's meal time.

THE FOUR SECOND RULE – *THAT'S RIGHT - FOUR*

In State-run motorcycle safety programs, we are taught that when riding in a group it's good to space ourselves out by one to two seconds. I suppose that's nice but frankly I get a little fed up watching riders in my rear view mirror, seeing the group unsafely bunch up in corners without enough space for everyone to effectively execute a proper delayed apex maneuver safely.

So one day I pulled my riding group over and went

back to the rider behind me. I began the conversation by applauding him on his group riding abilities to stay a few seconds back and stay staggered. I then noted that by doing things the way they teach us in an approved motorcycle safety class wasn't allowing him to have the best ride. He agreed. I suggested he get four seconds behind me and see if anything changed. He was happier and so was I. Now we were having a great time.

By putting four seconds between you and the rider in front of you allows you to have all the room you need to pick your line and enter and exit corners in a single file. At the same time you won't fixate on the rider in front of you and can maneuver obstacles much easier. You are riding your own ride rather than someone else's.

It also allows the rider in front of you to feel less pressure to keep moving by always seeing a rider directly behind in the rear view mirror.

But someone might get lost? No. As long as each member knows to pause at the next critical turn until they make eye contact with the rider behind them before turning (also known as leap frogging) no one is going to get lost.

PAVEMENT CHANGES

The Gorge area covers several counties. Each county maintains their own pavement. This means that pavement can change in an instant from sweet asphalt to gritty chip seal at the instant of a

Riding this close together is truly a recipe for disaster. Where would you escape if you were in the middle and needed to avoid a potential obstacle?

94

county line. Or vice-versa.

There are also sections where the road can change to gravel with little advance warning. It's a common occurrence on Forest Service roads, throughout the Northwest and elsewhere. If you're planning to ride a street bike on Forest Service roads, use a good atlas such as those produced by Benchmark Maps to determine if your proposed route is doable on a street bike. All pavement routes in this book were verified 100% pavement at the time of publication.

THE DELAYED APEX AND TWO OTHER CORNERING TECHNIQUES

There is a lot of information available concerning cornering technique and use of the Delayed Apex technique. Essentially if a rider goes wide in a turn and crosses over the center line this typically indicates the rider started the turn on the inside of the lane close to the shoulder.

Over the years, the Delayed Apex technique has been developed and refined by riding skills masters like David Hough. The concept is to begin your turn on the opposite side of the lane in the direction you plan to turn – i.e. begin a right turn near the center line, begin a left turn near the shoulder line, then focus your line of travel toward the inside edge of the turn reaching the inside of the corner just past the midway point of the turn. Didn't comprehend what I said? Read it again slowly and imagine the layout.

For more details, there are three things you can do. Pick up a copy of David Hough's Proficient Motorcycling, search the term 'motorcycle delayed apex' on the internet, or discuss the topic with someone who understands it already.

Another critical technique that will keep you out of

trouble in the turns is looking through the turn. If you've ridden motorcycles for a while, you've no doubt heard the term 'look where you want to go, not where you're going.' Eye's up and looking to the next place you're headed will help keep you from having a low side crash because your eyes went to the wrong place.

Keeping your eyes level is also essential to staying on course. As you turn your motorcycle and lean into the turn, your head will have a tendency to go on the same angle as your lean. But you brain is better suited for making the calculations of your next move if you keep your head level and don't lean or tilt it into the turn.

Combine these three techniques together (if you don't already) and you will most likely find yourself having much more fun in the twisties and doing it with more confidence.

THROTTLE/BRAKING CONTROL

There are reams of verbiage about throttle and braking control. If you've never studied the topic, start with the initial basic concept. It's a good idea to get your braking done before you enter a turn. If you're still braking in the corner there could be two reasons for it. The first is the most common – you've entered the corner too quickly. Doing so can lead to the bike sliding out from under you and leaving you in a bit of pain.

The other reason could be that you understand the more complex ways to utilize brakes and throttle together in cornering to reduce weight transfer between the front and rear of the motorcycle. For someone interested in moving their skills toward an advanced level, this is one method worth checking out more, but won't be covered here.

96

BIKE SWAPPING

Not the same as wife swapping, but the results can sometimes be just as disastrous. On more than several occasions we have seen crashes that involved bike swapping. The reason is obvious: rider gets on a bike they are unfamiliar with and attempts to do more than they are comfortable with on a strange steed. The next thing that occurs is often a low side or high side crash. Not good. Think before you swap. Really.

GEAR UP

I'm impressed with the way people at our rally gear up. For the most part, attendees are dressed for the crash they don't plan to have and as a result injuries are reduced greatly for those who do go down.

But that's not the norm. In fact, in a recent study we found that 83% of riders in the Northwest aren't dressed for the crash. They may be wearing tennis shoes, blue jeans or one of those helmets that looks more like a soup bowl. Let's look at what proper riding attire is in this new day and age where technology and economics make it affordable for everyone to dress for the crash.

Start with the helmet. You like your chin? If you don't wear a full face helmet, seriously consider upgrading to one. Those half shell and three-quarter shell helmets will do little to protect your face and chin if you launch off your bike unexpectedly. They take a little getting used to, but once you've worn one a few thousand miles you'll feel naked with anything less.

Riding jacket. A good riding jacket should have CE rated armor at the elbows, shoulder and over your spine. Levi, letterman and stylish bomber jackets do not. CE rated armor can often mean the difference between having a broken or fractured bone in a crash or not. In a minor crash having CE rated armor often means the rider will walk away from the crash with little pain. Without it your chances of injury can greatly increase.

Riding pants. Ditto on the jacket sermon above. Add chaps (horsey pants) to the list of gear that doesn't come with CE rated armor. Hey if you want to protect your legs, and why wouldn't you, might as well get some decent protective gear. But there is the question about "why wouldn't you" and the reasons are varied. Too hot, too sticky, too stuffy, too bulky are a few of the common ones. The solution is simple. Wear only a wicking base layer under your riding pants and all these symptoms disappear. Blue jeans and other cotton pants are the cause of these symptoms once you dump them you'll be far more comfortable in a pair of CE rated riding pants.

The boots are a start but there's plenty of road rash to be had for these two if they come off the bike today. All the gear, all the time.

Gloves. The choices are many. Look for gloves that offer good protection across the knuckles and palms. Garden gloves don't. When travelling for long distances, carry three sets at all times. A light set for riding in the heat, a medium set for typical days and a heavy set for fierce rain and cold moments. Regardless of the weather when you leave, you'll often be glad you've taken all three each time you ride.

Boots. Not tennis shoes, not sandals, not Birkenstocks, not cross trainers. When you ride you can greatly reduce your chance of injury to your ankle and feet by wearing a quality pair of over-the-ankle boots specifically designed for motorcycling. A stiff ankle area means you're less likely to twist your ankle in a crash and for those who have done that very thing, they may be happy to tell you the dramatic details of their recovery. It's no fun.

ADDITIONAL READING
- Proficient Motorcycling, David Hough
- More Proficient Motorcycling, David Hough
- Street Strategies, David Hough
- Sport Riding Techniques, Nick Ienatsch
- Total Control, Lee Parks

Blue jeans or camo pants will do little to protect your legs in a crash. Photo by RJ Myrup (rjs-s.com)

100

Tips and Tricks

Having spent many days riding in The Gorge, these tips and tricks are based on my observations from a motorcyclist point of view. Certainly riding a motorcycle is a bit different from car touring in terms of why you're doing it on two wheels, how to deal with weather and more.

WATER

Humans need to consume a lot of water each day. When you ride a motorcycle, your body is getting more water wicked away mile per mile than when you drive a car, so you need to drink more than normal if you're on the bike all day, especially when the heat is on. On a hot day, eight to sixteen ounces of water every few hours of riding isn't out of the question. Water helps regulate your body temperature and protect you from dehydration. Too much hydration though can leach away important electrolytes so moderation is the best policy.

EAR PLUGS

Shameless plugs, how about ear plugs? If you're not wearing them when you ride, you're going deaf slowly but surely. Low frequency wind noise over a long period of time will deteriorate your hearing moving you one step closer to tinnitus, a continual ringing in the ears. Earplugs can be purchased at any drugstore or from our Sound *RIDER!* online store (www.soundrider.com/store). Look for the soft foam type with a 30db rating or higher.

PACK THE SUN SCREEN

Even if you're riding around in full leather or textile gear, your face and neck are getting beat by the sun. Bring sunscreen with an SPF of 30 or higher and apply it as needed. I often wear an air-style suit when I ride in the summer months, which only has an SPF of about 4, so I coat my arms and legs too.

BUGS

Mosquitoes like to live in The Gorge from late spring into early summer, so be sure to pack the bug juice. Higher deet ratings means longer lasting.

EXERCISE

Sitting on a motorcycle several hundred miles a day can wreak havoc on the body. It's a good idea to get into a simple exercise regiment before, during and after taking a long trip. By sitting on a bike for several hundred miles in a day, lactic acid settles into the joints and I've found aspirin to have little effect on relieving the pain. Pulling out every hour or so and stretching will also lessen the effects of your body tightening up on the bike. Charlie -horses at 60 miles an hour are no fun. Protect yourself against them and the after effects of riding several days by exercising routinely. A book called Getting in Shape (Random House) has a lot of simple routines you can do at home or while on the road. One of my favorites is called the *Hotel Room Workout*.

RIDE EARLY

Some of my best rides have been between 6 a.m. and 9 a.m. The traffic is low, the sun is just coming up and the general light is lovely in the early morning hours throughout The Gorge. The sun rises in The Gorge just about 6 a.m. in the summer months – if you're camping you'll probably be awakened by the change in light, so take advantage of it and hit the road.

RIDE WITH THE SUN AT YOUR BACK

It's best to route your rides around the time of day and position of the sun so you're not continually riding into the sun in the early morning or late evening hours. As an example, a westerly ride on SR-14 in the early evening means you'll probably get the sun in your eyes. Couple that with a possible 25 mile an hour head wind and you've got your work cut out for you. Instead plan your rides with the sun at your back.

As an example, the Mt. Hood Loop described in this book is best done clockwise beginning in the morning. The light is on the mountain as you ride around it throughout the day. The BZ Boogie trip described in this book is best done in the mid-day giving you good light in Klickitat Canyon and illuminating Mt. Adams as you enter Glenwood.

If you have to ride east in the morning, consider using I-84 as it's got quite a bit of shade in the early morning hours before the sun makes its way overhead in the later hours.

ALWAYS PACK RAIN GEAR

Even if it doesn't rain when you're here, rain gear can help keep you warmer if you ride in the cooler early morning hours.

Typically it rarely rains more than 2 inches in a wet month (as opposed to the average 6"-8" in Seattle) and in the summer months rain is almost non-existent. I've awakened to a sunny morning, ridden during a wet afternoon and gone to bed under a clear sky - all on a day in July. Pack the raingear and you'll be better safe than sorry.

MAKE A BASE CAMP

If you plan to spend several days riding in The

Gorge, make a base camp in one location, rather than spending the night in a different spot each night. This will allow you to stow the gear you don't need each day in your tent or motel room and lighten up your bike for those tasty twisties you're going to be loving.

THE FUN IS IN THE TURNS

Tearing down I-84 at ninety miles an hour will do little to thrill you, the drivers around you or the State Patrol. Look to the turns on the smaller roads to be where the fun will be had. There are hundreds of turns in The Gorge when taken at the legal speed limit that will satisfy even the best riders.

DO IT AGAIN

As I've pointed out several times in the book, if you hit a stretch of road you like, by all means turn the bike around and ride it again and again until you've had your fill. You're in The Gorge for recreational pleasure so recreate over and over.

BRING A CAMERA

Be sure you pack a camera on the trip. There are many great photo opportunities you will come across during your ride through the region. Don't miss any.

REVERSE THE ROUTE

Okay, routing your ride in tandem with the rotation of the sun makes things more light friendly, but if you want to take a route in reverse, by all means go for it. It's like taking an entirely different route as you'll soon find out. This is why I suggest you ride the Mosier route in both directions.

See & Do

You could spend all day just riding your motorcycle around The Gorge, or you could get off your lazy butt and explore the fascinating places and things it has to offer. I suggest you do both. Simply plan your trip and slip an attraction or two into each day while you're here. Here are a few of my favorites.

Maryhill Museum

35 Maryhill Museum Dr, Goldendale, WA
(509) 773-3733

Originally intended to be Sam Hill's home, this stunning two-story work of architecture now houses both regular and traveling exhibits. It's hard to imagine such quality art can be found out here in the sticks. Food can be had in the café on the first floor. Not to be missed. Located along SR-14 just west of US-97.

The Stonehenge Replica

East of US-97 on SR-14, Goldendale, WA

Sam Hill left his mark in the region in many ways. Here you'll see a full-size replica of Stonehenge without the deterioration you'd see on the original in the British Isles. Built as a war memorial for World War One veterans, the structure provides an interesting perspective of places around The Gorge. It's a popular

Several hundred Valkyries gather at the Stonehenge replica to celebrate the summer solstice

106

place for pagans during equinox and solstices. Bring your camera.

Vista House

On US-30 just east of Corbett, OR

A stunning beauty perched above The Gorge with some outstanding views. Beautiful European architectural styling incorporates the foundation right into the road. The sweeper around the house is quite a treat on a bike. Multnomah and 5 other waterfalls can be seen from the stretch of highway leading upward to the House from exit 35 off I-84.

Goldendale Observatory

Goldendale, WA (509) 773-3141

The middle of nowhere makes a great spot for a telescope, especially a high powered one. This one features a 24 ½ inch reflecting Cassegrain lens and is open to the public. Telescope opens after 8p.m. and the trip makes a good late night ride. To get there, take SR-14 East to Lyle and head NE on SR-142. Once you arrive in Goldendale, turn left on Columbus and go north to the Goldendale Observatory State Park.

Columbia Gorge Interpretive Center

990 SW Rock Creek Dr, Stevenson, WA (800) 991-2338
Lots of information about The Gorge, its geological and cultural backgrounds, development of the river and more. Why is the world's largest rosary collection housed here?

Beacon Rock

SR-14 @ North Bonneville, WA
Just off SR-14 is a large rock popping up from The Gorge floor. Park your bike in the visitors lot, put on some light walking shoes, lock up your gear and climb to the top for a magnificent view looking eastward and westward through The Gorge.

Tom McCall State Preserve

US-30 at Rowena Crest, OR
This preserve, operated by the Nature Conservancy, is located at the top of Rowena Plateau. There are hiking trails and interpretive signs pointing out the flora and fauna as well as the geology of the area. A nice place to take a break as you tour US-30. Keep your boots on as the area has several rattlesnakes in residence.

Sternwheeler Riverboat Tour

Marine Park, Cascade Locks, OR (541) 374-8427
Step aboard this paddle boat and tour the area in style. Great views of The Gorge from a perspective available no other way. Boat leaves from Marine Park at the Cascade Locks (which has a short but interesting history of its own).

Hood River Museum

Port Marina Park, Hood River, OR (541-386-6772)
Follow this history of Hood River to the present.

Bonneville Lock & Dam
West of Cascade Locks off I-84, OR (541) 374-8442
　　One of the major power plants on the Columbia River, Bonneville features two well-done visitors' centers that include visible fish ladders. It's so big you can take separate trips to both the Oregon and Washington sides.

Maryhill Winery
9774 SR-14, Goldendale, WA (877) 627-9445
　　One of the top wine producers in the state is located here along SR 14 just West of Highway 97. After receiving many awards, they've made a good thing better by completing construction of a large amphitheater that is set right in the midst of the vines, below the well-decorated tasting room.

Gorge Discovery Center
5000 Discovery Dr, The Dalles, OR (541) 296-8600
　　Located along I-84 in The Dalles, on the Oregon side of The Gorge, the Center has all the answers about how The Gorge was formed by geologic forces and floods, its people through the ages and development of transportation through this area.

Route 30 Classics & Roadside Refreshments
1100 First Ave, Mosier, OR (541) 478-2525

　　A nice stop in Mosier, this museum/ice cream parlor houses some nice Porsche memorabilia and car stuff in general. Cool off with a soda or ice cream before you continue your ride.

Where to Eat

I routinely ride into the Columbia River Gorge and spend days at a time there. In fact my first trip was back in the summer of 2000. Since then I've dined at nearly every place there is to hit between Washougal and Goldendale, Troutdale and The Dalles. I know the good spots and I know the bad ones. If you don't see a place listed here it's either a) lousy, or b) it hasn't been open long enough to stand the test of time (three years in my book). So when I visit, where do I go you might wonder? These are the places I return to again and again and here's why. We've attempted to list them by city from West to East.

Black Rabbit Restaurant (aka McMenamin's Edgefield Manor)

In the world of riding there are two sides to the Black Rabbit - morning and evening. Let's start with morning.

The Black Rabbit is an excellent jumping off point for a trip up to Mt. Hood or into The Gorge. Located east of Portland on Old Highway 30 this former 'poor house' is now a dainty hotel, The Edgefield, with a nice restaurant inside. For breakfast, the Black Rabbit boasts a fairly consistent array of favorites from pancakes, pastries, egg dishes, breakfast meats and porridges as well as all the right juices and caffeine. It's hard to believe I've been dining here ten years now.

At night the Black Rabbit, along with its other fuzzy associates on the Edgefield grounds, becomes a 'pour house' making it a perfect ending to a long day on the road. What do I mean? Indeed my friends if you plan to visit the Edgefield in the evening and imbibe, do yourself a favor and book a room here beforehand. Do not plan to ride away. The grounds of the Edgefield feature 21

110

holes of golf and no less than 9 locations for purchasing a drink. Thus there's no need to go to Portland for a pub crawl when you can do it right here and birdie at the same time. And the evening menu at the Black Rabbit reads like a what's-what in British fare and beyond. Experience it at night – preferably, without your motorcycle. Cigars are welcome at select locations along your route (at least until Oregon instates a no-smoking law).

Black Rabbit Restaurant
2126 SW Halsey St
Troutdale, OR 97060
(503)492-3086
www.mcmenamins.com/index.php?loc=114

Multnomah Falls Lodge

As of this writing (2008) their website has not been updated in eight years, but of course their menu and prices have been. It's an awesome spot you won't want to miss. The most visible of the many waterfalls along historic Highway 30 as you travel between Troutdale and Cascade Locks; Multnomah Falls is so grand it sports a few parking spots, a gift shop and even an espresso bar. Head upstairs for a first rate meal and you might even consider a night's stay in the quaint lodge. Looking for a big breakfast? Stop in for the Sunday brunch!

Multnomah Falls Lodge
50000 Historic Columbia River
Bridal Veil, OR 97010
(503) 695-2376
www.multnomahfallslodge.com

Joe's El Rio Mexican Grill

With his success at the Big River Grill, proprietor

Joe Schlick set out to corral his Mexican food fancy with El Rio, located just across the from the Big River Grill in Stevenson. The menu here is fairly stable, so much so that I get many of the same items I enjoyed on my original visits back in 2000.

Joe's El Rio Mexican Grill
193rd SW 2nd St
Stevenson, WA 98648
(509) 427-4479
www.joeselrio.us

Big River Grill

Joe Schlick opened the Big River back in the 1990s. Well aware that the logging industry was taking a plunge, Schlick saw to it that the town of Stevenson would migrate more toward being a destination location for travelers rather than hang its hat on a dying timber trade. Thus the Big River Grill put into place the highest end menu the city had ever known and continues to serve up quality dishes today at fair prices. Décor? You wanna see a stuffed sturgeon that's 10 feet long (short for some of the big boys who lurk in the Columbia River) - get in here.

Big River Grill
192 SW 2nd St
Stevenson, WA 98648
(509) 427-4888
www.bigrivergrill.us

Walking Man Brew Pub

Owner Bob Craig shares his love for beer and food with his Walking Man brew pub. Craig spends his days focusing on top blends of hops and at nights provides his favorite pub dishes to accompany the resulting brews. Spring, summer and fall months allow guests to dine hop-side and train-side on the one-of-a-kind exterior/patio. Once you've experienced the Walking Man Brew Pub you will a) never look at a cross walk sign quite the same way again and b) wonder why there's men's and women's restrooms.

Walking Man Brewing
240 SW 1ˢᵗ St
Stevenson, WA
(509) 427-5520
www.walkingmanbrewing.com

The Crab Shack

There's only one way to dine at the Crab Shack… on the patio…and you may have to wait. The views of the Columbia River, the serenity of being in The Gorge, the peacefulness (until that dang train blows by) is well worth an evening spent at the Crab Shack. This is not to say that an evening inside won't produce a good meal, but for the same amount of money we'd rather be lounging outdoors getting our money's worth. Menu recommendations? Oh – get the crab by all means.

The Crab Shack
130 SW Cascade Ave
Stevenson, WA 98648
(509) 427-4400
www.nwcrabshack.com

Bahma Coffee Bar

Every big little town needs a good coffee bar and for Stevenson Bahma is it. Oh sure – the coffee is good so what makes it a happening place beyond that? For starters, the décor is like no other. You'd think the crew from Trading Places blew in with lots of inexpensive add-ons that truly do spruce up the place. Beyond that though, the breakfast and mid-day/night food offerings are exquisite for a place in the middle of a town of 5,000. Enjoy the breakfast sandwiches if you're just heading out in the morning, or the wide array of panini's if you're just passing through mid-day.

Bahma Coffee Bar
256 SW 2nd St
Stevenson, WA 98648
(509) 427-8700
www.bahmacoffeebar.com

Skamania Lodge

Starting a ride from the Stevenson/Cascade Locks area? Then this is a fine start for a breakfast buffet meal on a weekday. Beyond that it's all up to you. At this upscale resort, dinner menu items may not appear as they seem. Our experience says classy items like beef tenderloin and prime rib may be mid-grade at best. Until further notice, when it comes down to dinner save your money and dine down the hill in Stevenson instead.

Skamania Lodge
1131 SW Skamania Lodge Way
Stevenson, WA 98648
(800) 221-7117
www.skamania.com

Bonneville Hot Springs & Spa

Ahhhh…. – really! One of the few resorts in the world that pumps fresh hot spring mineral water right to the outdoor patio of your room. But how's the food? Unless you were a guest here you'd hardly know the place existed, but an ample meal to start or end your riding day awaits just beyond the main lodge area. They serve lunch too. Here's a wild idea…route this one into your mid-day ride schedule and enjoy a soak in their open-to-the-public hot spring facility. Oh yeah!

Bonneville Hot Springs & Spa
1252 East Cascade Drive
North Bonneville, WA 98639
(509) 427-9711
www.bonnevilleresort.com

Timberline Lodge

It's just an excuse to go for a ride… and a good one at that. The fare is always great here and the views, history and ambience can't be beat. Especially when you hearken back to those days of Jack Nicholson's 'The Shinning.' Oh - excuse me - you didn't see the movie? Go to Timberline Lodge, then rent the DVD or get it on the cable. Anyhow, Timberline Lodge could easily be a central location for a week of riding in the lower Cascades. For now (at least until retirement) we just like to think of it as a great place for food as we make our way around Mount Hood.

Timberline Lodge
Timberline Highway
Uninc Clackamas County, OR 97028
(503) 622-7979
www.timberlinelodge.com

Ice Axe Grill

Looking for an alternative to dining up at Timberline Lodge? The Ice Axe Grill is run by the same folks in a more pub sort of way. Nothing too incredible, just a very nice down home atmosphere that caters to those who want something more than a Sysco burger after a long day on the slopes. But in the less snowy seasons that might be us - the motorcyclists. Quality fare at a fair price.

Ice Axe Grill
87304 E Government Camp Loop
Government Camp, OR 97028
(503) 272-3172
www.iceaxegrill.com

Bear Creek Café

It's nothing fancy but the Bear Creek Café makes a nice lunch stop when you're in the Trout Lake area. The food is good and those Huckleberry shakes are a rare treat worth stopping in for. We also like the babbling irrigation brook just outside and if the temps are right you can dine at the picnic tables next to the brook.

Bear Creek Café
2376 SR 141
Trout Lake, WA 98650
(509) 395-2525

Andrew's Pizza

Two locations to serve you. It started in Hood River and had a baby in Stevenson. It's tasty pizza that rivals any chain, godfather or puck. Something about the dough, which must be a secret recipe, and yet the flavor continues on through the toppings as well. Good thing I only visit The Gorge now and then, otherwise I might get hooked.

Andrew's Pizza
310 SW Second St.
Stevenson, Washington
(509) 427-8008

107 Oak St
Hood River, OR 97031
PH: 541-386-1448
www.skylighttheater.com

3 Rivers Grill

One of the nicest views in Hood River, the 3 Rivers Grill looks across the Columbia River to the outlet for the White Salmon and Hood Rivers. Summer nights on the patio can be stunning as you dine and enjoy the sights of early evening wind surfers on the water. It's an upscale spot so bring your wallet.

3 Rivers Grill
601 Oak Street
Hood River, OR 97058
(541) 386-8883
www.3riversgrill.com

Brian's Pourhouse

Just across the street from the 3 Rivers Grill you'll find Brian's Pourhouse, but don't let the name fool you - it's more than a place for a drink. Our food experiences here have been exceptional with plenty of tasty tapas and entrees on the menu in a diverse format to satisfy just about everyone.

Brian's Pourhouse
606 Oak Street
Hood River, OR 97031
(541) 387-4344
www.brianspourhouse.com

Egg Harbor Café

The place for a substantial breakfast in Hood River, Egg Harbor makes a good meet-up point for group rides and you can usually find a spot to park just out front. The view out the window is a nice one of Mt. Adams. Breakfast basics abound; it's a menu with plenty of choices.

Egg Harbor Café
1313 Oak St
Hood River, OR 97031
(541) 386-1127
www.eggharborcafe.com

Horsefeathers Brew Pub

After a long day on the road, the Horsefeathers Brew Pub can help take the edge off. Up you go to the top of the hill with one of the nicest views we've ever seen from inside such an establishment. As you might expect, pub fare is what's on the menu and there's plenty of pours and bottles to choose from as well.

Horsefeathers Brew Pub
115 State Ave
Hood River, OR
(541) 386-4411

Maryhill Museum Café

If you're planning a trip to this world-class museum (really it is) then keep in mind there's no need to grab lunch anywhere else. The Maryhill Museum Café dishes up great sandwiches and even sports a few of the local wines on the menu to enhance your museum experience.

Maryhill Museum Café
35 Maryhill Museum Drive
Goldendale, WA 98620
(509) 773-3733
www.maryhillmuseum.org

Bluebird Inn

There's a lot of history at the Bluebird and getting there is a kick. It's one of the oldest taverns in Washington State, serves up decent American fare and sports one of the oldest Brunswick pool tables on the planet dating back to 1884.

Bluebird Inn
121 E. Market St
Bickleton, WA
99322
(509) 896-2273

Where To Stay

There are many choices for overnighting it in The Gorge. I like to pick a spot and stay there several nights so I don't have to move each day, instead spending my time riding the great roads here. You can choose from basic camping, inexpensive motels, bed and breakfast options or upscale spas. As a return visitor I tend to mix it up and do something a little different each time around.

CAMPING

When we talk camping I'm only including places that have full amenities such as showers, flush toilet restrooms and access to electricity for recharging your batteries, phone or running a hair dryer. As for primitive sites we don't include them here, but a good guide like the Benchmark Road & Recreation Atlas' for Washington and Oregon will tell you plenty.

Port of Cascade Locks Marine Park

Just across from Stevenson on the Oregon side of the Columbia River, you'll find the Port of Cascades

Locks Marine Park. The camping is located on the west end of the park. Showers are a bit of a walk to the east end and restrooms are down below at the boat ramp. Bring your walking shoes to be sure. The small island across the water is accessible by bridge and makes a nice stroll once you've set camp. Be sure to check out the view of the Bridge of the Gods from its western most tip. Interpretive signage here offers a history lesson in how the locks came to be.

Port of Cascade Locks Marine Park
355 WaNaPa St
Cascade Locks, OR 97014
(541) 374-8619
www.portofcascadelocks.org

Tucker County Park

Situated right alongside the Hood River as it flows toward the Columbia,Tucker County Park has been a favorite of mine for years. The park features tent sites under the trees or under the stars. It's one of the few camping areas in The Gorge that's train free, so don't expect any late night jolts from engineer Bill. On the other hand there is a rifle range nearby so you may awake in the morning to some popping sounds. Camping sites feature electricity, water and grills.

Tucker County Park
Hood River Valley, Hwy 81
Cultural/History exhibit, Oregon, 97031
1-800-547-7842

Maryhill State Park

For an easterly stay, you can pitch a tent or park an RV at Maryhill State Park. But don't say we didn't tell you so –

when the wind picks up here it can be fierce and many a rider has had to work hard to keep their tent from blowing away. The area is open, right on the river and situated below the Stonehenge Replica at the corner of US97 and SR14.

Maryhill State Park
50 US Hwy 97
Goldendale, WA 98620
(509) 773 5007
www.parks.wa.gov

MOTELS

Econolodge

Not always the case with every Econolodge, but this one has an AAA rating. On occasion I have seen them allow riders to park their bikes in the walkway behind the office.

Econolodge
40 NE 2nd St
Stevenson, WA 98648
1-800-359-4827

Best Western Cascade Locks

It's a Best Western. You get what you get – a step up from the Econolodge of course.

Best Western Cascade Locks
735 W Wanapa St
Cascade Locks, OR 97014
541/374-8777
www.bestwesternoregon.com/hotels/best-western-columbia-river-inn/

BED & BREAKFAST/INNS

McMenamins Edgefield Inn

Looking for a place to hang your helmet a few days with a little charm? The Edgefield Inn has it. In fact you could forego a day of riding during your stay here and take advantage of the Inn's restaurant offerings, large grounds and theater. You won't be able to park right outside your room and guests are encouraged to bring in their valuables. We love this place for breakfast at the Black Rabbit restaurant before jumping off for a ride.

2126 S.W. Halsey St.
Troutdale, OR 97060
(503) 669-8610
www.mcmenamins.com/index.php?loc=3

Columbia Gorge Riverside Lodge

A quaint B&B located right on the river and just across the tracks from the Walking Man Brew Pub in Stevenson it offers reasonable prices, but you won't find any TV's or in-room phones here. The owners kindly provide earplugs at your bedside when you arrive. You will more than likely want to use them.

200 SW Cascade Avenue
Stevenson, WA 98648
(509)427-5650
www.cgriversidelodge.com

UPSCALE

Bonneville Hot Springs

The hot springs that run just beyond the back door of this world class spa resort have been tapped and piped into the pool area and many of the upstairs rooms. Some riders stay here several days and keep the bike parked for at least one day to take a spa break.

Bonneville Hot Springs
1252 East Cascade Drive
North Bonneville, WA 98639
(509) 427-7767
www.bonnevilleresort.com

Skamania Lodge

No hot springs here but plenty of scenery and amenities including golf if you managed to get the clubs on the bike otherwise, just enjoy all the great art inside and their full service restaurant and bar facilities.

*Skamania Lodge
1131 SW Skamania Lodge Way
Stevenson, WA 98648
(800) 221-7117
www.skamania.com*

Columbia Gorge Hotel

One of the oldest accommodations in The Gorge is also one of the most upscale. It features old world charm and comes off almost European. The Farm Breakfast every Sunday is a historical brunch tradition.

*Columbia Gorge Hotel
4000 West Cliff Drive
Hood River, Oregon 97031
(800) 345-1921
www.columbiagorgehotel.com*

Timberline Lodge

Not exactly in The Gorge, but within striking distance of many great rides, Timberline Lodge is a great place to stay during the summer months when the air is warmer and the skiers have gone.

*Timberline Lodge
Timberline Highway
Unincorporated
Clackamas County, OR 97028
(503) 622-7979
www.timberlinelodge.com*

Creating Poker Runs in The Gorge

If you're not familiar with what a poker run is, here's the basics.

In the classic game of poker, each player is dealt five cards. The person with the best hand wins. Couple this with a nice motorcycle ride and you've got yourself a genuine poker run.

The event begins when you check in and receive a score sheet and route map. Typically there are five checkpoints along the route and you will draw a card at each one. It will then be noted on your score sheet and you will ride on to the next checkpoint. And like a game of poker, the person with the best hand at the end will be deemed the winner. Then the arguments may ensue that a full house is a higher score than a royal flush and on and on.

Bickleton Boogie Poker Run 2006
Presented by Sound RIDER!

NAME:_____

Sound *RIDER!*

The Northwest's Ultimate Motorcycling Resource
www.soundrider.com

rights. riding. racing.
SANCTIONED

	Amount	Punch
Checkpoint #1 Skamania Fairgrounds Open Times: 10 am - 11 am		
Checkpoint #2 Union 76, Goldendale 1103 East Broadway Open Times: 11:30 am - 1 pm		
Checkpoint #3 Blue Bird Inn, Bickleton 121 E Market St Open Times: 12:30 pm - 2:30 pm		
Checkpoint #4 Maryhill Loops Rd Open Times: 2 pm - 5 pm		
Checkpoint #5 Skamania Fairgrounds Open Times: 4 pm - 7 pm		
TOTAL		

These events are often used as fundraisers for various causes. Routes typically average from fifty to two hundred miles in distance.

Poker runs are a great way for groups of people to enjoy riding in The Gorge. You can use many of the loop rides in this book to run an event, or link a few routes together to create your very own. In fact some of the loop rides in this book evolved out of poker run routes over the years.

When creating a poker run in The Gorge, it's best to insure there are fuel stops at least every hundred miles. Certain models such as a Harley-Davidson Sportster or Suzuki SV650 get thirsty sooner than others and need to hit a gas station about that often.

Also be sure to plug a food stop in around lunch time. Places like Trout Lake, the Maryhill Museum and Timberline Lodge serve the purpose very well.

Bathroom breaks need to be considered as well. On one route between Mt. Hood and Corbett there were no bathrooms in between the two points so it was important to point that out in the ride notes ahead of time. Of course there's always one or two who don't read them and get stuck taking care of business along the side of the road.

In planning our poker runs, we strive to have them be scenic throughout. It would be easy to send someone into the forest for a day without seeing much. A little homework goes a long way in getting them to a beautiful overlook they can write home about.

In some states poker runs are frowned upon by the local gambling commission. If your poker run is all a game of chance you may be scrutinized. Do like we do and incorporate a game of skill into a checkpoint or two. We call this 'stupid checkpoint tricks' and it may involve a dart toss, trivia questions or riding skills. A game of skill will often keep the legal beagles at bay.

For more information on creating your own poker run, Google the search term 'sound rider poker run.'

RIDE INDEX

Rides are in bold and noted:
(p) = paved, (d) = dualsport

Barlow Trail, 18
Bickleton, 48
Bluebird Blast (p), 48
Bull Run, 18
BZ Boogie (p), 38

Clackamas River, 44
Cook/Underwood, 40
Cooper Spur Road, 44
Corbett, 19
Cougar Rock (d), 57, 60

Glenwood, 38, 40
Goldendale, 22, 48
Goldendale Observatory, 22

Hood River, 44, 69, 72, 77
Hood South (p), 44

Ice Caves, 74
Indian Heaven (d), 80

Klickitat Canyon, 22, 38

Lava Love (d), 74
Larch Mountain (p), 30
Lolo Pass, 72
Lyle, 38

Mabton, 48
McClellan Lookout, 26, 34, 80
Mosier Loop (p), 14
Mt. Adams Runabout (p), 40
Mt. Hood Scenic Loop (p), 18

Mt. St. Helens, 26, 34
Multnomah Falls, 18, 30

Old Dalles Road (d), 77

Panorama Point, 18, 69, 77

Rowena Curves, 14

Stabler, 57, 60, 66, 74, 80, 82
Sunset Falls (d), 60

Three Corner Rock (d), 66
Three Rivers Dualsport (d), 82
Three Rivers Loop (p), 26
Timberline East (d), 69
Timberline West (d), 72
Timberline Lodge, 18, 69
Trout Lake, 40, 74
Twisties Dinner & A Star Show
(p), 22

Vista House, 18, 30

Washougal River, 26, 82
Wind River Road, 26, 34
Windy Ridge/Mt. St. Helens
(p), 34

Yacolt Burn, 57